Cambridge Elements ≡

Cambridge Elements in International Economics
edited by
Kenneth A. Reinert
George Mason University

THE RMB IN THE GLOBAL ECONOMY

Yin-Wong Cheung
University of California

CAMBRIDGE
UNIVERSITY PRESS

CAMBRIDGE
UNIVERSITY PRESS

Shaftesbury Road, Cambridge CB2 8EA, United Kingdom

One Liberty Plaza, 20th Floor, New York, NY 10006, USA

477 Williamstown Road, Port Melbourne, VIC 3207, Australia

314–321, 3rd Floor, Plot 3, Splendor Forum, Jasola District Centre, New Delhi – 110025, India

103 Penang Road, #05–06/07, Visioncrest Commercial, Singapore 238467

Cambridge University Press is part of Cambridge University Press & Assessment, a department of the University of Cambridge.

We share the University's mission to contribute to society through the pursuit of education, learning and research at the highest international levels of excellence.

www.cambridge.org
Information on this title: www.cambridge.org/9781009236423

DOI: 10.1017/9781009236461

© Yin-Wong Cheung 2022

This publication is in copyright. Subject to statutory exception and to the provisions of relevant collective licensing agreements, no reproduction of any part may take place without the written permission of Cambridge University Press & Assessment.

First published 2022

A catalogue record for this publication is available from the British Library.

ISBN 978-1-009-23642-3 Paperback
ISSN 2753-9326 (online)
ISSN 2753-9318 (print)

Cambridge University Press & Assessment has no responsibility for the persistence or accuracy of URLs for external or third-party internet websites referred to in this publication and does not guarantee that any content on such websites is, or will remain, accurate or appropriate.

The RMB in the Global Economy

Cambridge Elements in International Economics

DOI: 10.1017/9781009236461
First published online: October 2022

Yin-Wong Cheung
University of California
Author for correspondence: Yin-Wong Cheung, cheung@ucsc.edu

Abstract: This Element discusses the global role of the RMB. After recapitulating its economic and trade growth experiences, we recount China's evolving exchange rate policy in the post-reform era, review the debate over whether the RMB is overvalued or undervalued, present China's policies to globalize the RMB, describe offshore RMB trading, assess the current global status of the RMB, and discuss geopolitical tensions in the last few years. Since 2009, the process of globalizing RMB has not been smooth sailing and has progressed quite unevenly over time. Despite the strong performance in the early 2010s, the RMB is underrepresented in the global market and its global role does not match China's economic might. The path of RMB internationalization is affected by both China's economic performance and geopolitical factors.

Keywords: offshore RMB trading, global FX trading, global reserves, geopolitics, RMB valuation

© Yin-Wong Cheung 2022

ISBNs: 9781009236423 (PB), 9781009236461 (OC)
ISSNs: 2753-9326 (online), 2753-9318 (print)

Contents

1 Introduction

Since Deng Xiaoping, the then paramount leader of China, launched the "reforms and opening up" (*Gaige Kaifang*, 改革開放 in Chinese) policy in late 1978, the Chinese economy has advanced at a phenomenal rate. Between 1979 and 2020, the Chinese economy, in local currency real terms, grew 37-fold and delivered an average annual growth rate of 9%. Even though China has experienced uneven development patterns in different sectors – the progress in financial sectors, for example, is noticeably behind the manufacturing and trade sectors – it managed to transform its inefficient and almost autarkic economy into the second-largest economy and the largest trading nation of the world in less than four decades.[1] China's economic performance over the last forty years is a tough act to follow.

In the process of building up its global economic eminence, China has periodically modified its foreign exchange policy and gradually increased the role of market forces in determining the value of its currency, the renminbi (RMB). Before the 1990s, the world did not pay much attention to China's exchange rate policy and the RMB. The global community has put China's exchange rate policy under scrutiny after observing that its trade surplus and holding of international reserves increased dramatically after its admission to the World Trade Organization (WTO) in 2001. There is extensive debate on the RMB valuation and the prognosis of the role of the RMB in the global monetary system.

China's exchange rate policy reached a turning point when it stepped up its efforts to promote the international use of the RMB after the 2007–8 global financial crisis (GFC). Since then, the global economy has anxiously embraced the implications of a global RMB for the balance of power in the world financial market and the race for geopolitical supremacy. One salient accomplishment of China's effort to globalize its currency is the inclusion of the RMB in the IMF's Special Drawing Right (SDR) currency basket. On October 1, 2016, the RMB acquired official global reserve currency status and became the first developing country currency to join the SDR currency basket.[2]

The process of globalizing the RMB has not been smooth sailing, though. After a strong start in building up the RMB's global currency status, the progress stalled for a few years after 2015 due to unexpected changes in China's foreign exchange management, capital control measures, and geopolitical tensions that reduced the

---

[1] The United States is the largest economy. Based on purchasing power parity measures, China is the world's largest economy.

[2] The IMF announced the inclusion of the RMB in the SDR basket in November 2015. The US dollar, the euro, the Japanese yen, and the British pound are the four incumbent SDR currencies.

appetite for RMB activity overseas. Despite its impressive economic heft – as the second-largest economy, the largest holder of international reserves, and the largest trading nation – the RMB plays a relatively minor role in the global market. For instance, in 2020 China accounted for 17% of world output and 13% of international trade. At the same time, the RMB accounted for less than 3% of global reserves, less than 5% of global foreign exchange trading, and less than 3% of world payment currency.

The RMB's path to becoming a full-fledged global currency depends on China's economic conditions, its ability to gain the trust of foreign investors and geopolitical powers, and the reactions of incumbent countries, including the United States. It is useful to take stock of China's efforts and assess the role of the RMB in the global market, which would shed light on the prospect of a global RMB currency. We do not mean to determine the factor underlying the under-presentation of the RMB in the global financial system; instead, our discussion aims to provide a concise and balanced account and highlight the multitude of factors, including capital controls, policy uncertainty, and geopolitics, that affect a currency's global status. In Section 2 we recount China's evolving exchange rate policy in the post-reform era after recapitulating its economic and trade growth experiences. Section 3 reviews the debate on RMB misalignment and whether the RMB is overvalued or undervalued. Section 4 presents China's policies to promote the international use of the RMB and offshore RMB trading. Section 5 assesses the current global status of the Chinese currency. Section 6 discusses geopolitical development. Section 7 offers some concluding remarks.

2 Background

During its first three decades, the communist People's Republic of China was relatively isolated from the main global economy; it was proud of being "self-reliant" in building its economic and political structures. However, the Chinese economy was stuck at a low level of per capita gross domestic product (GDP) and was among the list of low-income countries. For instance, China's real per capita GDP ranked 115th in 1970.[3]

China's modern history of economic development reached a landmark when it officially endorsed the "reforms and opening up" policy directive in the 1978 National Party Congress.[4] Since then, China has pursued a gradualist approach

---

[3] World Bank data, via http://knoema.com/WBWDIGDF2015Aug/world-development-indicators-wdi-august-2015.

[4] The reform agenda advanced in the Third Plenum of the 11th National Congress of the Communist Party of China (December 22, 1978) advocated the so-called Four Modernizations – the modernization of agriculture, industry, science and technology, and the military. See, for example, Rosen (1999) and OECD (2005) for accounts of the open-door policy and its implications.

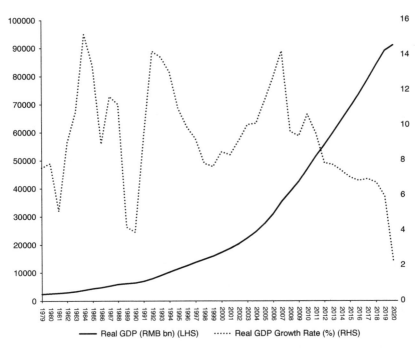

Figure 1 China's real GDP and growth rate in local currency, 1979 to 2020
Note: Data from the World Bank.

to opening up its economy. In the last few decades, it has transitioned from a lethargic, planned economy to a vibrant and growing one, and from a mostly closed economy to a significant player in the global market. The rest of this section highlights China's economic growth and trade integration, and recounts its evolving exchange rate policy.

2.1 Growth Powerhouse

Since 1979, China has experienced phenomenal growth, which is sometimes dubbed "the China economic miracle." Figure 1 shows China's real GDP and growth in local currency from 1979 to 2020. Despite the apparent wild swing in the early years and the slow-down in recent years, the Chinese economy had an average annual growth rate of 9.22% and grew 37-fold in the local currency in real terms.[5] Sometimes China's economic miracle is compared with the strong

---

[5] On the reliability of official growth data, see Fernald, Hsu, and Spiegel (2015), Holz (2004), Klein and Ozmucur (2003), Koch-Weser (2013), and Rawski (2001, 2002). China has revised GDP growth rates with data from its National Economic Census. Based on the conducted censuses, China revised its growth rate upward by 16.8% in 2004, 4.4% in 2008, 3.4% in 2013, and 2.1% in 2018.

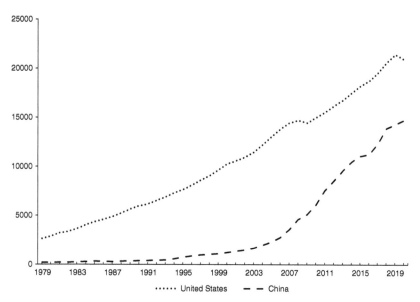

Figure 2 China and the US GDP in current billions of US dollars, 1979 to 2020

Note: Data from the World Bank.

growth record of, say, Japan in the post–World War II period and the Four Little Dragons in the 1970s to early 1990s.[6]

Comparing the Chinese and US growth experiences in US dollar terms is quite revealing. China's average annual growth rate was 11.69% between 1979 and 2020, 9.90% between 1979 and 2000, and 13.56% between 2001 and 2021. The corresponding US average annual growth rates are 5.23%, 6.72%, and 3.66%. The growth differential significantly narrows the gap between the sizes of the Chinese and US economies (Figure 2).

Figure 3 offers an alternative perspective on China's strong economic performance: it depicts the shares of world GDP accounted for by China and the United States. In 1979, China accounted for less than 2% of the total world GDP. By 2020, it had surpassed the 17% mark and was in a position to challenge the United States' 24.72%.

Despite starting at a low level in the 1970s, China's "super-charged" economy in the last four decades makes it a main growth engine of the global economy. There are discussions on China overtaking the United States as the world's largest economy as early as, say, 2030 (Economist, 2014; Pethokoukis,

---

[6] See, for example, Cheung, Chinn, and Fujii (2007a). Smith (2016) compares the Japanese and Chinese economies.

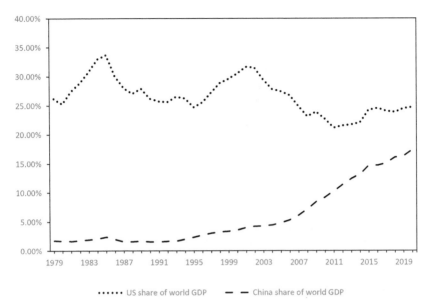

40.00%
35.00%
30.00%
25.00%
20.00%
15.00%
10.00%
5.00%
0.00%

1979 1983 1987 1991 1995 1999 2003 2007 2011 2015 2019

•••••• US share of world GDP   — — China share of world GDP

Figure 3 Shares of world GDP: China versus the US, 1979 to 2020
Note: Data from the World Bank.

2014; World Bank, 2013a). Indeed, when measured on the PPP-basis, in 2014 the Chinese economy overtook the United States to become the largest economy.[7] Despite the differing views on the relevance of market-based or PPP-based data, the prolonged high growth rate is an astonishing accomplishment for the Chinese authorities.

Mirroring its growth momentum, China's GDP per capita has delivered a strong performance since 1979 (Figure 4). In US dollar terms, China's output per capita shows an average annual growth rate of 10.69% between 1979 and 2020; its growth in the twenty-first century is higher than that of 1979–2020. China's growth rate compares favorably to the US average annual rate of 4.25 during the same period. The growth differential reduced the US to China GDP per capita ratio from a high of 63.45 in 1979 to 6.05 in 2020. China's per capita GDP has improved from less than 2% of the US figure in 1979 to 16.53% in 2020. Although China has caught up significantly, there is still room for improvement. China's per capita GDP in US dollar terms ranked 89th in 2020, according to World Bank data.[8] When the output is measured with PPP-based data, China's per

---

[7] Ruoen and Kai (1995) presented an early comparison of the Chinese and US GDP using PPP-based data. See World Bank (2013b) for further information about PPP data.
[8] https://data.worldbank.org/indicator/NY.GDP.PCAP.CD?most_recent_value_desc=true.

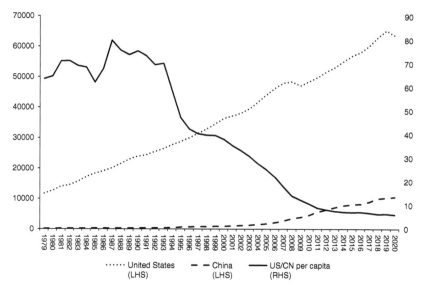

Figure 4 GDP per capita: China versus the United States, 1979 to 2020
Note: Data from the World Bank.

capita GDP in 2020 is 17,211 international PPP dollars, which is 27% of the US rate and ranks 95th worldwide.[9]

2.2 A Trade Titan

The 2013 news headline that China's total foreign trade (the sum of exports and imports) in 2012 surpassed the US total affirmed China's prominence in international trade. Before China overtook the United States, it had been the largest trading nation for more than six decades. China's fast expansion in international trade has been a significant driver of its phenomenal economic growth[10] and provided a strong base for designing the 2009 RMB internationalization policy based on cross-border trade settlement (see Section 4).

The early phase of the 1978 reform initiative focused on upgrading China's economy, and opening up has underpinned the expansion of its trade sector. China's accession to the WTO in December 2001, its success in attracting foreign direct investment that brought in the needed capital and technical know-how, and strategic positioning in the global production chain have provided additional catalysts to establish China's dominance in international trade.

---

[9] China's 1990 figure is 982 international PPP dollar which is 4.1% of the corresponding US figure; see
https://data.worldbank.org/indicator/NY.GDP.PCAP.PP.KD?most_recent_value_desc=true.

[10] Benkovskis and Wörz (2015), for instance, show that even allowing for the value-added and other issues of measuring trade performance, China's gain in global trade is substantial.

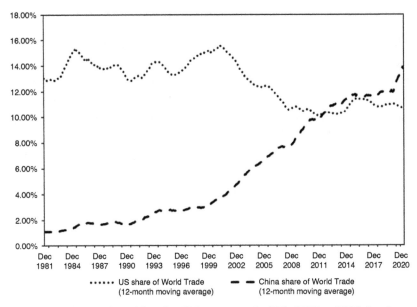

Figure 5 Shares of world trade: China versus the US, 1979 to 2020 (twelve-month average)
Note: Data on import CIF and export FOB in US dollars from the World Bank.

Figure 5 depicts the shares of global trade contributed by China and the United States between 1979 and 2020. The figure clearly shows that China's share has been increasing over time, while the US share has been declining since the beginning of the 2000s. Specifically, China's share of global trade was 1.10% in 1981, 3.63% in 2000, and 13.32% in 2020. The gain in share is noticeably more substantial after joining the WTO in 2001. On the other hand, the US share of global trade declined gradually from a high of more than 15% in 2000 to slightly more than 10% in 2020. China's gain in global trade share reflects its strong growth in total trade. Its foreign trade value multiplied 11 times between 1981 and 2000, and by an even more impressive 108 times between 1981 and 2020. The growth is much higher than the 7.43 times of the United States and the 8.98 times of the world between 1981 and 2020.

Between 1981 and 2020, China grew its imports by around 95 times and exports by 120 times. The growth was stronger again after joining the WTO in 2001. China has been the world's largest exporting country since overtaking Germany in 2009. On the import side, China was the second-largest importing country in 2020. The growth of exports outpaces that of imports, and the growth differential yields China's huge trade surplus over time. We will return to the differential growth in imports and exports in Section 3.

2.3 Exchange Rate Policy

China's official currency, the RMB, was introduced on December 1, 1948, before the official establishment of the People's Republic of China on October 1, 1949, and the yuan is its basic unit. Both political and economic considerations have guided China's exchange rate policy, though the relative weight of these two considerations has shifted over time. Before launching reforms in 1979, the policy was designed to support the central economic plan. Since 1979, the policy has gradually shifted toward economic factors and assigned market forces a more significant role in determining the RMB exchange rate. In this subsection, we offer a brief review of China's exchange rate policy after 1979.[11]

2.3.1 Early Phases: 1979 to 2004

The initial phase of China's reform, masterminded by Deng Xiaoping, focused on revamping the manufacturing and trade sectors and improving productivity and efficiency. China tested an export-led growth strategy to rejuvenate the economy in the process of transforming its economy. To facilitate the export sector and manage foreign exchange reserves, China experimented with alternative mechanisms to determine the RMB's value. Between 1979 and 1993, China practiced a dual (or, in practice, multiple) exchange rate regime that allowed for different degrees of market forces in different sectors of the economy.[12]

China made a substantial policy change in January 1994 when it replaced the dual-rate arrangement characterized by the official rate and the swap market rate with a single exchange rate, which was set at the level of 1 US dollar to 8.7 Chinese yuan (CNY). Figure 6 shows the nominal and the (reversed) real RMB exchange rate against the US dollar. Initially, the unified single market rate relative to the official rate represented a devaluation of about 33%. Then, the RMB gradually appreciated to the level of CNY 8.28 per US dollar and remained around that level until mid-2005, when China moved to a different exchange rate arrangement. The close link between the RMB and US dollar is also illustrated by their effective exchange rates. The Bank for International Settlements (BIS) data indicate that the nominal effective exchange rates of the

---

[11] Cheung, Chow, and Qin (2017), Liew and Wu (2007), Shi (1998), and Wu and Chen (2002) provide alternative accounts of the evolution of China's exchange rate policy. Miyashita (1966) discusses the early currency and financial systems.

[12] Huang and Wang (2004), Lin and Schramm (2003), and Xu (2000) review and assess China's exchange rate arrangements in the early stage of the reform period.

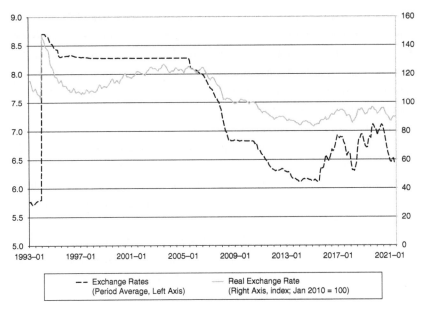

Figure 6 The nominal and real (reversed) RMB exchange rates against the US dollar

Note: Data from IMF.

RMB and the US dollar had a correlation coefficient estimate of 0.99 between January 1994 and June 2005.[13]

Conceivably, a stable RMB exchange rate provides China with an economic environment conducive to developing its economy and its trade sector. Indeed, the stable RMB/US dollar exchange rate served China well: China's trade surplus, economic growth, and holding of international reserves started their remarkable expansion between 1994 and 2005.[14] However, the drastic devaluation and the subsequent de facto peg to the US dollar have become the source of contentious debate on China's exchange rate policy. The United States, in particular, bitterly complained that China was pursuing a deliberate undervaluation policy to gain unfair advantages in international trade.

2.3.2 Revamping the Fixing Mechanism

Amid soaring trade surplus and criticisms about the de facto peg, China, on July 21, 2005, instituted a different mechanism to determine the daily official

---

[13] During the same period, the correlation of the real effective exchange rates of the RMB and the US dollar is 0.77.

[14] Ding (1998) and Schnabl (2013) note the problems underlying China's multiple rate regimes and the benefits of a stable RMB.

RMB fixing. The China Foreign Exchange Trading System (CFETS), which is housed in Shanghai and falls under the direct jurisdiction of the People's Bank of China, is responsible for implementing the fixing mechanism. Specifically, China adopted a managed and regulated floating exchange rate regime based on market demand and supply, and with reference to a basket of currencies (People's Bank of China, 2005).

Compared with the bilateral exchange rate peg against the US dollar, the valuation against a currency basket provides a better measure of the overall strength of the RMB. Further, a stable currency basket exchange rate policy can free the RMB from tracking the US dollar and offer China a leeway to play down the role of the US dollar in formulating its exchange rate policy.

The revamped policy started with a 2% revaluation against the US dollar from 8.28 to 8.11 on July 21. Then, the RMB experienced a gradual appreciation until July 2008 (Figure 6). Ma and McCauley (2011) assert that the arrangement is effectively a crawling peg. When the 2007–8 GFC began, China switched to a de facto peg – the RMB exchange rate was closely managed around the level of CNY 6.83 per US dollar from July 2008 to June 2010 (People's Bank of China, 2010).

On June 19, 2010, China essentially reinstated the 2005 managed and regulated exchange rate regime. The announcement was taken as an affirmation of the established policy of managed floating rate arrangement. Again, the authorities gave no official information on the component currencies and their weights in the currency basket. Understandably, China has more leeway to manage the exchange rate by not disclosing the specifics of the currency basket. The reinstated policy was in force until August 2015, when China made another main change in its exchange rate policy.

Despite the declared currency basket policy, the observed RMB movement suggests that China mainly managed the RMB against the US dollar – or assigned a very large role to the US dollar in the currency basket (Frankel, 2006, 2009; Funke and Gronwald, 2008; Sun, 2010). After reinstituting the currency basket arrangement in mid-2010, and before another policy change in August 2015, the correlation of the nominal effective exchange rates of the RMB and the US dollar was 0.87, and that of the real effective exchange rates was 0.76; both values indicate a high degree of association between the RMB and the US dollar.

Despite the close association, the RMB exhibited a higher degree of flexibility against the US dollar after the 2005 policy change (Figure 6). In addition to the exchange rate formation mechanism, China experimented with increasing RMB's flexibility. It widened the RMB daily trading band against the US dollar from an initial value of ±0.3% around the daily fixing to ±0.5% on May 21,

2007; ±1% on April 16, 2012; and ±2% on March 17, 2014.[15] The gradual widening of the trading band adds flexibility to the RMB exchange rate. While these changes signify its efforts to enhance the role of demand and supply forces, China has quite routinely reverted to capital controls and administrative measures to manage its exchange rate when the RMB is under undue market pressure.[16]

In the midst of continuously modifying its managed and regulated exchange rate regime, in 2009 China introduced the cross-border trade settlement scheme to initiate its RMB internationalization program. The scheme encourages using the RMB to denominate and settle cross-border trade transactions. The Bank of China (Hong Kong), which facilitates the designated cross-border RMB transactions, was appointed in 2003 as the RMB clearing bank in Hong Kong.

2.3.3 Enhanced Fixing Mechanism and the CFETS RMB Currency Basket

On August 11, 2015, China fine-tuned the RMB central parity formation mechanism that determines the official daily RMB fixing against the US dollar. The revamped mechanism determines the official daily fixing based on the closing rate in the previous day, market demand and supply factors, and the rates of other major currencies (People's Bank of China, 2015). This fine-tuning was meant to improve transparency and strengthen the role of market forces in setting the official daily rate. While the IMF endorsed the change as "a welcome step as it should allow market forces to have a greater role in determining the exchange rate," the United States stated that "the increased (RMB) flexibility is considerably less than is needed."[17] The global market was quite nervous about the RMB deprecation that accompanied the policy change – the RMB depreciated 1.9% against the US dollar on August 11, 2015, and a cumulative 4.4% in the first three trading days of the new fixing procedure. The degree of depreciation, which is relatively large and unexpected, stirred up unrest in the global financial market. Some countries, including the United States, worried that it was the beginning of a currency war.

---

[15] Ahmed (2009), Frankel (2006, 2012), Kawai and Liu (2015), Obstfeld (2007), and Prasad (2016) note that exchange rate flexibility helps China to achieve both internal and external balances, reduce its huge trade surplus, promote the international use of the RMB, and achieve monetary policy autonomy.

[16] Some studies on China's capital controls and their effectiveness and measurements are Chen (2013), Chen and Qian (2016), Cheung and Herrala (2014), Cheung and Qian (2011), Ma and McCauley (2008), and Prasad and Wei, (2007). Rebucci and Ma (2019) offer a recent survey on selected recent theoretical and empirical studies on capital controls.

[17] See www.imf.org/external/country/CHN/rr/2015/0811.pdf and the United States Department of the Treasury (2006).

On December 11, 2015, China posted the composition of the CFETS currency basket on the web[18] and reiterated the message of managing the RMB value against a basket of currencies.[19] Initially, the currency basket comprised thirteen component currencies: the US dollar has a weight of 26.4%, the euro 21.39%, the Japanese yen 14.68%, and the remaining currencies less than 10% each.[20]

Intuitively, the policy change will increase the transparency of the RMB fixing mechanism, lower the US dollar effect on RMB valuation, and hence improve the RMB stability. Cheung, Hui, and Tsang (2018a, b) study the official daily RMB fixing dynamics in the early phase of the enhanced fixing mechanism. These authors find that the RMB daily fixing against the US dollar is significantly affected by the onshore and offshore RMB exchange rates and the US dollar index. However, the US dollar index effect in the post-August 2015 period is less than that observed in the pre-August 2015 period. The effect of the CFETS RMB currency basket index can be detected after controlling for offshore RMB volatility effects. In a sense, the enhanced fixing mechanism has weakened but not eliminated the dependence on the US dollar.

Since disclosing the composition of the CFETS currency basket in 2015, China has adjusted the basket composition four times. On January 1, 2017, China expanded the CFETS currency basket from thirteen to twenty-four component currencies (China Foreign Exchange Trade System, 2016). Since 2017, China has further adjusted the weights of the twenty-four component currencies of the basket three times; these adjustments were effective on January 1, 2020, January 1, 2021, and January 1, 2022. Table 1 lists the weights of the component currencies of different vintages of the CFETS RMB index.

China reduced the weight of the US dollar from 26.4% to 18.79% in the first three adjustments and increased it marginally to 19.88% in January 2022.[21] Strategically speaking, the expanded CFETS currency basket and weight adjustments dilute the US dollar role in setting the central parity and, purposely, drive the market focus away from the bilateral US–RMB exchange rate. These moves reduce the US dollar influence on the RMB and China's international trade and finance. Because changes in the component currencies of the basket are one of the factors determining the daily fixing against the US dollar, the

---

[18] The RMB indexes based on BIS and SDR weights are included for comparison purposes.

[19] See the commentary posted on www.pbc.gov.cn/english/130721/2988680/index.html.

[20] The remaining ten currencies are HKD (6.55%), GBP (3.86%), AUD (6.27%), NZD (0.65%), SGD (3.82%), CHF (1.51), CAD (2.53%), MYR (4.67%), RUB (4.36%), and THB (3.33%).

[21] The combined weight of the US dollar and currencies pegged to it (Hong Kong dollar, United Arab Emirates dirham, and Saudi riyal) was reduced from 32.95% (December 2015) to 26.78% (January 2021) before being upped to 27.29% in January 2022.

Table 1 Compositions and weights of the CFETS RMB currency basket

	January 1, 2022	January 1, 2021	January 1, 2020	January 1, 2017	December 11, 2015
USD	0.1988	0.1879	0.2159	0.2240	0.2640
EUR	0.1845	0.1815	0.1740	0.1634	0.2139
JPY	0.1076	0.1093	0.1116	0.1153	0.1468
HKD	0.0346	0.0359	0.0357	0.0428	0.0655
GBP	0.0313	0.030	0.0275	0.0316	0.0386
AUD	0.0571	0.0589	0.0520	0.0440	0.0627
NZD	0.0061	0.0063	0.0057	0.0044	0.0065
SGD	0.0302	0.0312	0.0282	0.0321	0.0382
CHF	0.0076	0.011	0.0144	0.0171	0.0151
CAD	0.0217	0.0226	0.0217	0.0215	0.0253
MYR	0.0444	0.0431	0.0370	0.0375	0.0467
RUB	0.0366	0.0385	0.0365	0.0263	0.0436
THB	0.0335	0.0319	0.0298	0.0291	0.0333
ZAR	0.0121	0.0147	0.0148	0.0178	–
KRW	0.0967	0.0988	0.1068	0.1077	–
AED	0.0167	0.0169	0.0157	0.0187	–
SAR	0.0228	0.0271	0.0216	0.0199	–
HUF	0.004	0.0035	0.0037	0.0031	–
PLN	0.0105	0.0097	0.0084	0.0066	–
DKK	0.0046	0.0041	0.0040	0.0040	–
SEK	0.0061	0.0061	0.0058	0.0052	–
NOK	0.0037	0.0026	0.0021	0.0027	–
TRY	0.0082	0.0072	0.0073	0.0083	–
MXN	0.0206	0.0211	0.0198	0.0169	–

Note: Column 1 lists the currency codes in the Index. Weights of individual currencies of different vintages of the currency basket are presented under their effective dates in the first row.

volatility of RMB fixing may have to increase with the reduction in the US dollar weighting to achieve the objective of stabilizing the RMB index,

On May 27, 2017, China tweaked the central parity formation mechanism by adding a "counter-cyclical factor" to the fixing procedure.[22] That is, in addition to the previous closing rate and the overnight variation of the currency basket

---

[22] In February 2017, China shortened the reference period of the currencies used in calculating the central parity from 24 to 15 hours. The reduction was meant to better reflect changes in the forex market.

value, the fixing is affected by the countercyclical factor.[23] This factor is meant to alleviate procyclical herd behavior and reduce volatility. Unlike the other two factors determining the fixing, China gave only a general guideline for the countercyclical factor, but not how it is calculated and its weight in setting the parity rate. The opaqueness of the countercyclical factor favors the discretionary component of the central parity formation mechanism and affords China extra room to manage and set the daily fixing.[24] The countercyclical factor was suspended on January 10, 2018, re-introduced on August 1, 2018, and suspended again on October 27, 2020.

This brief review does not do justice to China's efforts to achieve RMB flexibility and convertibility, albeit in its own style, so as to promote allocative efficiency and support economic growth. Since 1994, China has made numerous policy changes to strengthen the role of market forces and enhance exchange rate flexibility. The reform has not progressed smoothly and has gone through a "two steps forward, one step back" process in response to domestic and foreign conditions. The August 2015 reform was a bold move to unshackle the RMB exchange rate. However, the periodic backpedaling detracts from China's efforts to liberalize its financial markets. Apparently, by tweaking the exchange rate mechanism, China wishes to design an appropriate exchange rate policy that ensures stability, rather than the RMB being "correctly" valued at the time. Given China's enormous size and increasing links to the global economy, the world will continuously monitor its exchange rate policy and its spillovers to the global market.

3 RMB Misalignment

Exchange rates are a main conduit connecting a country's economy to the global market. They affect trade competitiveness and capital flows between countries. Misaligned exchange rates can lead to domestic and cross-border resource misallocation, global imbalances, and distorted capital flows, which can damage the stability of the global financial system and the international economic order (Benassy-Quere, Lahreche-Revil, and Valerie, 2008; Cline and Williamson, 2010; Morrison and Labonte, 2013). In the past few decades, there have been recurrent complaints about countries manipulating their exchange rates to gain unfair trade competitiveness and expand their exports markets to support economic development. Such a policy imposes economic

---

[23] Technically, designated banks/dealers submit to CFETS fixing quotes with their own countercyclical adjustment factors. CFETS then determines the daily fixing.

[24] Su and Qian (2021) show that the countercyclical factor weakens the explanatory power of the currency basket factor, and the onshore and offshore RMB exchange rates.

costs on others and on the global system. China is the most recent large country that is accused of benefiting from artificially depressed value of its currency.

While exchange rate misalignment is a rather standard concept, it can be empirically challenging to determine if a currency is misaligned and, even less likely, to agree on the degree of misalignment. Hinkle and Montiel (1999) offer an early discussion of issues on defining and measuring exchange rate misalignment. At the risk of oversimplification, a currency is misaligned when its exchange rate deviates from its equilibrium value. Different notions of the equilibrium exchange rate would thus generate different assessments of misalignment.

The poor performance of empirical exchange rate models presents another challenge to evaluating exchange rate misalignment. The infamous Meese and Rogoff puzzle casts doubt on the ability of empirical models to describe exchange rate movements (Meese and Rogoff, 1983). Specifically, it is difficult to find a commonly agreed framework to model different exchange rates across different historical periods and, hence, assess equilibrium exchange rates. The general conclusion of this seminal study is mostly affirmed by subsequent analyses (Cheung, Chinn, and Pascual, 2005; Cheung et al., 2019; Engel et al., 2019; Rossi, 2013).

The debate in the last two decades on RMB misalignment aptly illustrates the challenges of assessing exchange rate misalignment, and the empirical studies are prone to misleading narratives. The international attention on RMB valuation stems mainly from China's extraordinary export competitiveness and rapidly expanded holding of international reserves at the onset of the twenty-first century. The typical "graphical evidence" that the RMB is substantially undervalued in the early twenty-first century is shown in Figure 7, which plots China's trade balance (per GDP) and holding of international reserves. China's trade surplus was relatively steadfast in the 1990s, increased sharply in the 2000s until reaching a high point of 10% of GDP in late 2008, then experienced a decrease associated with the 2007–8 GFC before resuming growth. During the same period, China's holding of international reserves exploded from the level of US$21 billion in 1993 to a high of US$4 trillion around mid-2014 before fluctuating around the low US$3 trillion level. China's startling buildups in trade surplus and holding of international reserves have put its policy objective of exchange rate stability under scrutiny.

When China maintained a stable exchange rate of around 8.27 during the 1997 Asian Financial Crisis, it was acknowledged as a desirable one that avoided competitive devaluation and promoted regional economic stability. However, the similar stable exchange rate policy has been deemed the source of China's unfair competitive edge in international trade. China's efforts in revamping its foreign exchange policy, including the modification of the RMB central parity formation mechanism in August 2015, have not silenced its critics. China's trade partners,

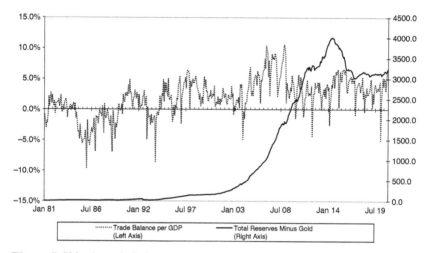

Figure 7 China's trade balance per GDP and holding of international reserves: January 1981 to December 2020

Note: Data from IMF.

especially the United States, frequently blamed China for their large trade deficits and global imbalances because of its RMB undervaluation policy.[25] Even when the IMF, in its May 2015 Article IV consultation mission press release (International Monetary Fund Communications Department, 2015) stated that the RMB is at a level that is no longer undervalued but urged China to make "rapid progress toward greater exchange rate flexibility," the US Treasury Department, a few hours after the IMF press release, offered a different opinion and reiterated its assertion that the RMB was still substantially undervalued.[26]

The US concern about China's exchange rate policy is reflected by its repeated threats over the past two decades to label China as a currency manipulator. The recent formal accusation happened in 2019, when the United States officially labeled China a currency manipulator.[27] Previously, the "currency manipulator" label had been applied to China in 1992 and 1994 (United States Department of the Treasury, 1992, 1994, 2019). China considers the RMB policy part of China's domestic economic sovereignty, which foreign forces should not interfere with. The typical official stance is that China does not

---

[25] As early as 2002, Masajuro Shiokawa (the then Finance Minister of Japan) complained about China's exchange rate policy.

[26] The findings of Almås et al. (2017), Cheung, Chinn, and Nong (2017), and Cline (2015) corroborate the IMF "no longer undervalued" assessment.

[27] Some observers attribute the 2019 currency manipulator label to the China–US geopolitical dispute (Section 6).

manipulate the RMB exchange rate for competitive purposes and always maintains the rate at a basically stable manner around the equilibrium level.[28]

With its growing importance in the global market, if China manipulates its currency there will be serious economic and political backlashes. The extensive policy debate on RMB valuation in the last two decades attests to the contentious nature of assessing whether China is manipulating its currency. The debate has triggered numerous studies on RMB misalignment. Studies in the 2000s usually favored the view that the RMB is undervalued, if not seriously undervalued (Bergsten, 2007; Coudert and Couharde, 2007; Frankel, 2006; Funke and Rahn, 2005; Goldstein and Lardy, 2009; Wang, Hui, and Soofi, 2007). Based on the undervaluation estimates available at that time, the 2005 Schumer–Graham bipartisan bill proposed to impose a tariff rate of 27.5% on all imports from China to force China to cease currency manipulation.[29]

An overarching question is: given the difficulty of defining equilibrium exchange rate and modeling exchange rate, especially for currencies of transitional economies, how confident we are in determining whether the RMB is misaligned and its precise degree of over- or undervaluation? Under the well-known overshooting model (Dornbusch, 1976), when the observed exchange rate is different from the long-run equilibrium rate, it can be consistent with market fundamentals. That is, the equilibrium path of the exchange rate can deviate from its long-run value in the short run, and observed misalignment does not necessarily imply a disequilibrium scenario that requires policy remedies.

Besides the uncertainty associated with the equilibrium exchange rate, a few studies raised concerns about the sensitivity of RMB misalignment estimates to the empirical model, assumptions, data choices, and statistical methodologies used to generate these estimates. It is difficult to assess the precise degree of RMB misalignment when there is a lack of a consensual exchange rate model and the estimate is sensitive to assumptions underlying empirical specifications.

Cheung, Chinn, and Fujii (2007b) point out that sampling and estimation uncertainties should be incorporated in assessing the significance of RMB misalignment estimates. Dunaway, Leigh, and Li (2009) and Schnatz (2011) showed that equilibrium real exchange rate estimates and misalignment estimates are sensitive to even small changes in assumptions underlying model specifications, explanatory variable definitions, and sample periods. The RMB estimate can imply severe undervaluation or overvaluation depending on the

---

[28] See, for example, the speech by the PBoC Governor Yi Gang in 2019: www.pbc.gov.cn/gou tongjiaoliu/113456/113469/3870187/index.html.

[29] http://schumer.senate.gov/SchumerWebsite/pressroom/press_releases/2005/PR4111 .China020305.html.

assumptions. Fischer and Hossfeld (2014) pointed out the sensitivity of misalignment inferences to different productivity measures. Almås et al. (2017) and Cheung, Chinn, and Nong (2017) showed that nonlinearity plays a role in estimating RMB misalignment in addition to data sample and model specification.

In the past two decades, studies with different theoretical and empirical specifications of the equilibrium exchange rate, different sample periods, and different estimation methods have generated numerous RMB misalignment estimates that span a wide range of overvalued and undervalued estimates. To assess what can be learned from the plethora of empirical studies, Cheung and He (2022) collected 3,108 RMB misalignment estimates from 95 studies to conduct a meta-analysis using a Bayesian model averaging framework.[30] In principle, the meta-analysis allows the pooling and aggregation of information from these studies. The large-scale study identifies, for example, that the choices of time series vs non-time series data and cointegration vs noncointegration technique have significant implications for RMB misalignment estimates. Their results indicate that the empirical RMB undervaluation estimates are characterized by a high level of uncertainty and do not offer a conclusive statistical inference on RMB misalignment.

Conceivably, the "common" wisdom of a "severely" undervalued RMB feeds off China's heavily managed RMB and its fast buildups of current account balance and international reserves. The United States, for example, propagates the belief that "China has a long history of pursuing a variety of economic and regulatory policies that lead to a competitive advantage in international trade, including through facilitating the undervaluation of the RMB" (United States Department of the Treasury, 2018, p. 3). Ambivalent empirical evidence of RMB undervaluation does not lend unambiguous support for the political rhetoric. The inconclusive result is in accordance with the well-known difficulty of measuring the equilibrium real exchange rate and quantifying the (statistical) uncertainty surrounding exchange rate misalignment estimates.

The foregoing discussion should not be interpreted as supporting the notion of *no* RMB undervaluation. Instead, we foreground the difficulties and limitations of empirical exercises that prevent us from making a sharp and precise inference. With a diverse set of misalignment estimates, one can always find some empirical estimates to substantiate the view of an undervalued or overvalued RMB. Both academics and policymakers should exercise caution in interpreting empirical RMB misalignment estimates and asserting their

---

[30] Bineau (2010) and Korhonen and Ritola (2011) present two early meta-analysis of RMB misalignment estimates. See also Cheung and Wang (2020).

relevance in policy debate. Specifically, it is crucial to understand factors that can affect empirical RMB misalignment estimates to avoid unintended consequences in policymaking.

4 RMB Internationalization

In the last few decades, China has astounded the world with its reform policies and the dynamic expansion of its economy and international trade. Because the reform initially prioritized the real economy development over financial markets, China has a relatively underdeveloped financial sector. However, the flourishing economy and international trade call for accompanying reforms in financial markets. Since its accession to the WTO in 2001, China has gradually restructured its domestic financial markets and exchange rate policy.

The advent of the 2007–8 GFC hastened China's efforts to promote international use of the RMB. Following the scheme of cross-border trade settlement in RMB in 2009, China introduced other policies, including bilateral local currency swap arrangements, RMB clearing bank assignments in offshore markets, and channels for accessing RMB-denominated assets. Since then, global attention has gradually shifted from debating RMB valuation to the RMB's evolving role in the global market and the implications for the international monetary architecture.[31]

Similar to other reform areas, government policies play an essential role in shaping the path of RMB internationalization. Consistent with its revealed preference for reform gradualism and stability, China has strategically internationalized the RMB with a mix of state-led initiatives comprising administrative control measures and market-driven forces. China schematically promotes using the RMB to facilitate cross-border trade transactions, followed by trade, financial, and investment transactions in regional, international, and global markets.

Buttressed by its economic prowess and trade dominance, China's RMB internationalization scored a substantial payoff in 2015 when the IMF announced that it would include the RMB in its basket of SDR currencies. In addition to endorsing China's currency reform efforts, the IMF decision confers upon the RMB the official role of an international reserve currency. This is a symbolic boost to the RMB's credibility and enhances its global acceptance.

---

[31] Some studies on RMB internationalization are Chen and Cheung (2011), Chen and Peng (2010), Cheung, Ma and McCauley (2011), Eichengreen (2013), Eichengreen and Kawai (2015), Frankel (2012), Lai (2021), Prasad (2016, 2017), and Subacchi (2016). These studies offer alternative perspectives of motivations, promotional policies and their effectiveness, and implications for domestic and global economies. Garber (2017) present a general discussion of geopolitics and the euro and the RMB, the two ascending global currencies.

Conceivably, inclusion in the SDR could increase the demand for RMB-denominated reserve assets by central banks or institutions that passively or actively hold SDRs in their portfolios.

After reaching the 2015 high point, the process of globalizing the RMB has progressed quite unevenly and, in some areas, has even reversed. The change occurred in parallel with China's heightened (administrative) foreign exchange management, financial deleveraging policies, and the concurrent increase in global uncertainty and geopolitical tensions that have decreased global demand for RMB-denominated assets. Further, the eruption of the China-US trade dispute and the subsequent change in the view toward China do not favor the international use of the RMB. The 2020 coronavirus pandemic presented China with another chance to regain the momentum of globalizing its currency. The pandemic impacted China hard in the first half of 2020; however, with its effective public health control measures, China demonstrated its economic resilience in late 2020 and 2021.[32] This speedy economic recovery and the RMB's stability have improved the attractiveness of RMB-denominated assets to international investors and enhanced the global usage of the RMB.

In the following subsections, we recount China's main policies for promotion of RMB internationalization and discuss its outsourcing practice – the offshore RMB trading. China's RMB internationalization program covers and interacts with a wide range of topics. While a complete coverage of RMB internationalization is beyond the scope of this study, we offer an overview.

4.1 Promoting RMB Internationalization

It is commonly perceived that China kick-started its concerted efforts to internationalize its currency with the 2009 scheme of cross-border trade settlement in RMB.[33] The scheme sets up the institutional arrangements for using RMB to settle international trade transactions.[34] At that time, it was a policy response to the severe US dollar liquidity shortage that occurred during the 2007-8 GFC and which seriously disrupted global trade. Settling trade in RMB allows China to reduce its reliance on vehicle currencies, including the US dollar, to conduct international transactions. Further, cross-border trade settlement in RMB promotes

---

[32] China's (dynamic) zero-Covid policy is a resource-intensive one that involves mass testing and large-scale lockdown. The extra-contagious Omicron variant of 2022 has raised concerns about the economic and social toll and the sustainability of the strict (dynamic) zero-Covid policy.

[33] The RMB cross-border trade settlement arrangement in, say, 2003 (State Administration of Foreign Exchange of China, 2003a, b) was not directly relevant to the current RMB internationalization policy.

[34] Initially, the scheme covered designated companies in five pilot cities. Since August 2011, it covers all regions in China.

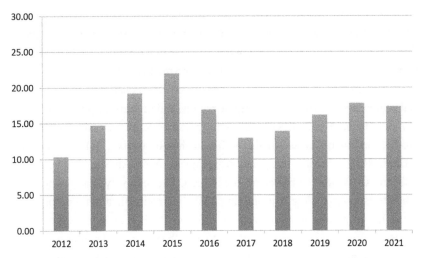

Figure 8 Share of China's trade settled in RMB (percentage)
Note: Data from CEIC.

the international use of the currency and helps Chinese companies to manage exchange rate risk.

China's international trade primacy provides a solid foundation to establish the RMB as a main trade settlement currency. Chen, Peng, and Shu (2009) and Cui, Shu, and Chang (2009), for instance, project that the share of China's trade settled in RMB is around one-third or 30%.[35] Nevertheless, due to inertia, it may take some time to realize the trade settlement role of the RMB.

Since the introduction of the 2009 cross-border trade settlement scheme, both the share and the volume of cross-border trade settled in RMB have exhibited impressive growth. For instance, the percentage of Chinese trade settled in RMB steadily increased to above 20% in 2015, then reversed slightly before moving back toward the 20% mark during the 2020 pandemic year (Figure 8).

4.1.1 Offshore RMB Clearing Banks

In December 2003, China allowed banks in Hong Kong to offer loans and deposits in RMB that are cleared via the Bank of China (Hong Kong), which was appointed as the local RMB clearing bank of Hong Kong. By creating an offshore RMB market in Hong Kong as a precursor to allowing designated financial institutions to conduct offshore RMB businesses, China prepared for

---

[35] Japan settled at most about 40% of its trade in the Japanese yen (Goldberg and Tille, 2008; Ito et al., 2010).

the cross-border RMB settlement infrastructure.[36] An RMB clearing bank outside China provides a crucial facility supporting RMB internationalization. The RMB clearing bank in Hong Kong that clears cross-border RMB transactions is the first facility of this kind outside the mainland of China.

Since then, China has strategically appointed RMB clearing banks in financial centers across different geographic regions and time zones. The assignment of a clearing bank indicates China's willingness to recruit the financial center to promote international use of the RMB. In the Appendix, Table A1 lists the offshore RMB clearing banks in chronological order. Among the twenty-six offshore RMB clearing banks, ten are in Asia. The relatively heavy concentration attests to Asia's role in promoting RMB internationalization. For instance, Hong Kong literally monopolized the offshore RMB settlement and clearing infrastructure in the first decade of the twentieth century and still accounts for the lion's share of offshore RMB business these days. China assigned London an RMB clearing bank in June 2014, and Toronto in November 2014. Thus, the core network of offshore RMB clearing facilities makes 24-hour, round-the-clock RMB settlement and clearing possible.

New York and Tokyo joined the network of offshore RMB clearing banks in September 2016 and October 2018. These two centers also have a local bank providing RMB clearing services. The timing of assigning RMB clearing banks is not consistent with the prominence of these two global financial centers. Conceivably, China's decision to set up an offshore RMB clearing arrangement depends on diplomatic and political factors besides economic considerations. The relatively late assignment of a local RMB clearing bank is probably due to critical views expressed by Japan and the United States regarding China's state-led trade and exchange rate policies.

The presence of a local RMB clearing bank opens up RMB business opportunities, reduces transaction costs, and offers liquidity in case of an RMB squeeze. However, a local RMB clearing bank is not critical for accessing offshore RMB clearing. Since 2004, foreign banks and corporations have had access to offshore RMB clearing through the RMB real-time gross settlement system in Hong Kong.[37] China's Cross-Border Interbank Payment System (CIPS), which was launched in October 2015, further reduces the practical role of offshore RMB clearing banks. Authorized by the People's Bank of China, CIPS is a specialized clearing system that works with direct participants

---

[36] While Hong Kong is legally part of China, it is considered an "offshore" market for RMB transactions.

[37] London, for example, has established itself as a prime offshore RMB center in Europe and, excluding China and Hong Kong, accounted for more than 50% of RMB foreign exchange transactions (SWIFT, 2013) before housing an RMB clearing bank in 2014.

and indirect participants to provide clearing and payment services for financial institutions in the cross-border RMB and offshore RMB business. Strategically, CIPS offers a platform to settle cross-border RMB transactions outside the US-dominated global payment infrastructure provided by the Society for Worldwide Interbank Financial Telecommunication (SWIFT). By 2021, CIPS had 75 direct participants and 1,187 indirect participants from more than 90 countries and regions on 6 continents.[38]

4.1.2 Bilateral Local Currency Swap Agreements

Besides establishing offshore RMB clearing facilities, China has negotiated bilateral local currency swap agreements with selected trading partners to shore up offshore RMB liquidity since 2008. The policy initiative provides a liquidity backdrop in the event of an RMB shortage to support cross-border RMB trade settlement. The agreement partner can obtain RMB funding through the swap from the People's Bank of China and use it to settle trade with China or as an emergency source of RMB liquidity. These bilateral swap agreements involve the RMB and national currencies of the counterpart economies, not the US dollar.[39] That is, economies with these agreements can bypass the US dollar and conduct trade and other cross-border transactions in their own currencies. By deploying these bilateral swap agreements, China reduces the influence of the US dollar on its trade activity and promotes the use of the RMB overseas.

The bilateral swap agreements signed between 2008 and the first half of 2021 are listed in Table A2 in the Appendix. The bilateral agreement typically has a maturity of three years, and is renewable.[40] Since December 2008, China has signed bilateral local currency swap agreements that amount to more than 3.99 trillion yuan with forty foreign central banks or monetary authorities (People's Bank of China, 2021). China creates an extensive network of bilateral RMB currency swap agreements to support and facilitate the international use of the RMB.

These bilateral RMB swap agreements are different from the swap arrangements signed under the Chiang Mai Initiative or between the United States and selected central banks during the financial crisis. These swap agreements are typically dollar-based arrangements designed to provide (precautionary) dollar liquidity in a crisis (Aizenman and Pasricha, 2010). The importance of ensuring global dollar liquidity is well illustrated by the swap arrangements offered by

---

[38] See www.cips.com.cn/cipsen/7050/index.html for additional information.

[39] In the past, the US dollar was the currency of swap agreements signed by China, say, under the Chiang Mai Initiative and the Multilateral Chiang Mai Initiative.

[40] The latest agreements with Korea, Hong Kong, Thailand, and Canada have a maturity of five years.

the US during the 2007–8 GFC and, again, the March 2020 financial crisis triggered by the coronavirus pandemic.

Garcia-Herrero and Xia (2015), Liao and McDowell (2015), and Lin, Zhan, and Cheung (2016) investigate factors that affect China's choices of bilateral swap agreements. These studies show that the choices of counterpart economies and swap line amounts are significantly influenced by both economic and noneconomic factors that include trade intensity, economic size, strategic partnership, and free-trade agreements, as well as corruption and political stability. Song and Xia (2020) show that the signing of bilateral local currency swap agreements promotes the use of RMB in settling the corresponding cross-border trade – a result that affirms the policy's objective.

4.1.3 Renminbi Qualified Foreign Institutional Investor Program

The principal functionality of offshore RMB clearing banks and bilateral RMB currency swap agreements is the provision of RMB liquidity to support cross-border trade and international transactions. Besides shoring up offshore RMB liquidity, China has contemplated several ways to beef up the demand for RMB-denominated assets and enhance the attractiveness of offshore RMB holdings.

In addition to investing in Dim Sum bonds, RMB-denominated equities, and exchange-traded and over-the-counter RMB derivatives in offshore markets, in December 2011 China launched the Renminbi Qualified Foreign Institutional Investor (RQFII) program for approved foreign institutions to invest offshore RMB in China's onshore financial markets. The RQFII program is a variation of the Qualified Foreign Institutional Investor (QFII) program introduced in 2002 that allows authorized foreign investors to invest with a foreign currency – usually the US dollar.

Similar to its previous RMB internationalization policies, China chose Hong Kong as a testing ground for the RQFII initiative. The first batch of authorized institutions of the initiative included only approved subsidiaries of China's brokerage houses and fund managers in Hong Kong, and they mainly invested in the Chinese onshore fixed income products such as bonds instead of equities. Since then, the RQFII program has expanded to include financial institutions in different offshore financial centers, and to cover asset classes beyond fixed income products.

Since launching the RQFII program, China has introduced a few other inbound investment schemes, including the Shanghai–Hong Kong Stock Connect in 2014, the Mutual Recognition of Funds Scheme in July 2015, the Shenzhen–Hong Kong Stock Connect in 2016,[41] North-Bound Bond Connect

---

[41] The Shanghai–London Stock Connect Program was launched in June 2019. As of August 2020, the London Stock Exchange listed two global depositary receipts (GDRs) under the program.

in July 2017 and South-Bound in September 2021, and Wealth Management Connect in September 2021. These "connect" programs enhance the connections between financial markets in China and Hong Kong, and the cross-border flow of RMB. Through these programs, foreign investors participate in designated onshore markets under specific regulatory frameworks via the financial infrastructure in Hong Kong. Foreign investors can participate in China's onshore financial markets through these alternative inbound investment schemes and the RQFII program. Compared with the RQFII program, each of these connect schemes individually offers a narrow scope of investable securities. Nevertheless, these inbound investment schemes compete with the RQFII program for foreign capital.

As well as introducing these alternative inbound investment schemes, China has implemented a few modifications of the RQFII program, including participant qualifications and eligible investment classes. On June 6, 2020, China implemented a major program change and removed the quota limits and restrictions on country/region of the RQFII program (State Administration of Foreign Exchange 2019a). In November 2020, China consolidated QFII and RQFII under the new Qualified Foreign Investor (QFI) program. Besides removing investment caps, the QFI program streamlines the application process, simplifies the paperwork, relaxes restrictions, and expands the investment scope. The QFI provides an improved environment for institutional investors to invest in China's onshore capital markets. These changes signal China's yearning for foreign institutional investments in its domestic financial markets and promoting the global stature of the RMB.[42]

4.1.4 Other Policy Measures

In the early 2010s, the three policies of offshore RMB clearing banks, bilateral RMB currency swap agreements, and the RQFII program (which was merged with QFII into the QFI program in 2020) were the three main tools for developing offshore RMB business and promoting RMB internationalization. In addition to these three measures, China has taken other steps to expand the international use of the RMB in trade and investment and nurture the global image of its currency.

The two listings are also available to international investors in Kong via the Shanghai–Hong Kong Stock Connect.

[42] There is no corresponding quota removal for the Qualified Domestic Institutional Investor (QDII) program, which governs Chinese residents' investments in foreign assets. By November 2021, the approved DQII quota is US$ 154 billion.

Commodity Pricing

The US dollar is the primary pricing currency of the global commodity market. Most actively traded commodities, including gold and oil, are quoted and transacted in the US dollar. The role of the United States in pricing globally traded commodities reflects and reinforces its preeminence in the international monetary system.

As part of its broad RMB internationalization policy, China has strategically introduced RMB-denominated contracts in commodity markets in which it is a significant player. With its extraordinary growth in global commodity trade (World Bank 2018), China has felt that its commodity trade activities are vulnerable to US dollar pricing. The promotion of RMB-denominated commodity contracts reflects China's yearning to reduce its reliance on US-dollar-based trading of commodities. It also offers RMB-denominated hedging tools to domestic investors and consumers. In addition to fostering global uses of the RMB, this strategy undercuts the US dollar's hegemony in the commodity space.

Against the backdrop that it is one of the biggest gold producing, consuming, and importing countries in the world, China has schematically developed its gold exchange. In September 2014, China opened its RMB-denominated gold bullion trading on the Shanghai International Gold Exchange, which is located in the Shanghai Free Trade Zone, to global investors. The Shanghai International Gold Exchange is a fully owned subsidiary of the Shanghai Gold Exchange and is known as the "International Board" of the Exchange.

Similar to other RMB internationalization policies, Hong Kong was chosen as the pilot economy to experiment with integrating the Chinese domestic and international gold markets.[43] In July 2015, the Shanghai and Hong Kong gold market connect initiative was launched to explore cross-border trade in gold and expand the strategy of RMB internationalization. The Shenzhen and Hong Kong gold connect was introduced in November, 2017.

In April 2016, the Shanghai Gold Exchange launched an RMB-denominated Shanghai Gold Benchmark Price or Shanghai Gold Fix. The Shanghai Gold Fix boosts the RMB gold-pricing power and signals China's stature in the international gold market. Futures contracts based on the RMB-denominated gold fix are offered in the Chicago Mercantile Exchange and the Dubai Gold & Commodities Exchange.

Crude oil is a crucial commodity for the global economy. Driven by its phenomenal growth, China's demand for energy, especially oil, has increased

---

[43] Since October 2011, the Chinese Gold and Silver Exchange Society in Hong Kong has offered RMB-denominated gold trading to both local and global investors.

substantially in recent decades. Since 2017, China has surpassed the United States in annual gross crude oil imports.[44] Given the strategic importance of crude oil, China is seeking a role in the global crude oil market. In March 2018, six years after its original planned launch date, China introduced its RMB-denominated oil futures contracts on the Shanghai International Energy Exchange. The so-called Shanghai oil futures contract is the first commodity derivative to be opened up to international traders.

The Shanghai oil futures contract has been quite well received. Soon after its introduction, the contract became the most traded oil futures contract in Asia and the third most traded in the world after the West Texas Intermediate Crude Oil futures contract trade on the New York Mercantile Exchange and the Brent crude oil futures contract traded on the Intercontinental Exchange. The quick advance of the Shanghai crude oil futures contract revives the discussion about the rivalry between the petroyuan and petrodollar. The development also supports the view that the contract could be a regional and possibly later a global benchmark, rivaling the established global benchmarks, including the Brent crude oil futures contract and the West Texas Intermediate Crude Oil futures contract.

In addition to the RMB-denominated gold and crude oil futures contract, foreign investors can participate in six other specific varieties of RMB-denominated commodity futures: iron-ore futures, pure terephthalic acid (PTA) futures, natural rubber futures, low-sulfur fuel futures, copper futures, and palm oil futures. Representing another step in opening up its financial markets, in June 2021 China introduced two RMB-denominated options contracts accessible by foreign investors; they are the palm oil and crude oil options.

Evidently, the development of these RMB-denominated commodity contracts is in accordance with China's growing importance in these commodity markets. Establishing its own commodity trading ecology helps China to consolidate its influence and assert its role in the global commodity market. For individual commodities wherein it has a significant presence, China has schematically pursued the gradualist approach to develop and introduce RMB-denominated contracts in these markets since the 1990s. Alongside other financial liberalization policies, this effort has gathered pace in recent years. With its own RMB-denominated market network, China enhances its pricing power in the global commodity market, secures its acquisition of commodities, challenges the US dollar's dominance, and strengthens the global stature of the RMB.

---

[44] China became the world's largest net importer of total petroleum and other liquid fuels in 2013.

International Initiatives

Apace with the development of policies facilitating the RMB's international uses, China pursues international initiatives that have the potential of building up the RMB's global status and raising its global acceptance. In the early 2010s, China intensified its campaign to be part of the IMF's SDR currency basket. The inclusion of the RMB in the SDR basket has been hailed as a triumph for China. The IMF's decision signals its endorsement of China's importance in the global economy and the global role of the RMB. The RMB is the first developing country currency included in the SDR basket. It also marks the first time the SDR basket added a new currency since the euro was launched in 1999.

The RMB officially joined the SDR basket on October 1, 2016, with a 10.92% weight. The weights of the other four SDR currencies are 41.72% for the US dollar, 30.92% for the euro, 8.33% for the Japanese yen, and 8.01% for the British pound. The official global reserve currency status recognizes China's global economic significance and acknowledges China's efforts to deepen reform and liberalize its financial markets. The admission to the SDR basket gives the RMB new opportunities to boost its global credibility and expand its global reach. In view of RMB's SDR status and its increased integration into the global financial system, international investors are enticed to direct their investments toward RMB-denominated assets. Inclusion in the SDR basket assures the RMB's role in the global market and has favorable implications for the global demand for the RMB.

Usually, the IMF reviews the composition and valuation of the SDR basket every five years. As such, the IMF should have assessed the role of the RMB and announced a new composition of weights in the SDR basket in 2021. However, the IMF postponed the assessment exercise to 2022. In May 2022, the IMF completed the SDR valuation review, maintained the composition of the SDR basket, and devised updated basket weights that will be effective on August 1, 2022. As expected, the RMB's weight is higher (an increase from 10.92% to 12.28%) in the updated basket.[45] Given China's growing influence on the global economy, it is expected that the RMB's weight in the SDR basket will increase gradually over time.

Besides pursuing SDR membership, China has crafted international initiatives that can expand the use of the RMB abroad. Two prime examples are the Belt and Road Initiative on infrastructure and trade and the Asian Infrastructure Investment Bank on financing infrastructure projects.[46] These initiatives are

---

[45] In addition to the RMB, the IMF increased the US dollar weight from 41.735 to 43.38%, and decreased the euro weight from 30.93% to 29.31%, the Japanese yen weight from 8.33% to 7.59%, and the British pound weight from 8.09% to 7.44%.

[46] See http://english.www.gov.cn/beltAndRoad/ and www.aiib.org/en/index.html.

intertwined with the RMB internationalization program. For instance, through outward RMB-denominated FDI and credit facilities, these initiatives can increase the use of the RMB overseas. Also, in the event that trade and infrastructure projects thrive among the member countries of the Belt and Road Initiative, there are incentives to fund these projects using the RMB to safeguard against financial risks.

Digital RMB

Since the initiation in 2020 of the testing phase of its digital RMB project, China has steadily expanded the scope and the scale of digital RMB usage.[47] The digital RMB entails a digital transaction platform that offers, among other benefits, low fees. China will gradually extend the originally designed domestic digital RMB infrastructure to cover cross-border transactions; one possible extension is to connect the domestic digit transaction platform to, say, the CIPS. Similar to the CIPS, such a development will facilitate cross-border and offshore businesses in the digital RMB. Conceivably, China's advanced digital RMB program could help to develop a new international monetary system that appeals to countries benefiting from China's growing economic and political influences or to countries looking for ways to bypass US financial sanctions.[48]

While a digital RMB could enhance the international role and the use of the RMB overseas, there are a few caveats. For instance, a digital RMB presents a technologically sophisticated form of the Chinese currency. An upgrade in transactional efficiency by itself, however, will make little difference to foreign investors' demand for the RMB if there are no accompanying improvements in, say, capital controls, exchange rate management practices, policy transparency, and geopolitical conditions. Further, there are concerns about the implications of using digital currencies within and across national borders. These concerns include consequences on financial stability, interoperability, privacy, and state surveillance. Cross-border digital currency transactions could affect monetary policy independence and the practical rights in accessing and using digital currencies and surveilling transactions across borders.

---

[47] See, for example, Assenmacher et al. (2021) for an analysis of the macroeconomic effects of central bank digital currencies, Kiff et al. (2020) for a recent survey of research on retail central bank digital currencies, Fernández-Villaverde et al. (2020) for the implications of a central bank digital currency for private banking business, and Working Group on E-CNY Research and Development of the People's Bank of China (2021) for developments in China's digital currency project.

[48] US financial sanctions against other countries are usually considered to be detrimental to the dollar's global role. However, Dooley et al. (2022) argue that sanctions, including the 2022 sanctions on Russia, strengthen the dollar's global dominance.

Given these caveats, it is not necessarily a foregone conclusion that the digital RMB can elevate the international role of the Chinese currency. The RMB's global status remains dependent on factors that affect the desirability of the currency, the confidence and trust of foreign investors, and the geopolitical conditions.

4.2 Offshore RMB Trading

After experimenting with offshore RMB transactions in Hong Kong, China has actively propagated similar offshore RMB businesses in other financial centers around the world. Typically, China uses Hong Kong as a laboratory for RMB internationalization policies and evaluates their operational issues and experiences before introducing them to other offshore financial centers.[49] Using this strategy, China "outsources" offshore RMB activity to advance RMB internationalization and, at the same time, maintain its control on capital flows and financial markets. By "outsourcing" RMB internationalization, China can assess the opportunities and challenges of a globalizing RMB and the implications for China's ability to manage the Chinese economy. Both Chinese and foreign market participants can gain practical experiences of conducting international business in the RMB in a legal environment recognized by international participants.

Do offshore markets contribute to the global status of a currency? The US dollar best exemplifies the point. The US dollar's preeminence bolsters full-fledged offshore US dollar markets around the globe, and these buoyant offshore US dollar markets validate the primacy of the US dollar. Consequently, the global dominance of the US dollar reinforces the US formidable economic and political clout.

Usually, the scale and scope of offshore usages of a currency are driven by market forces and demand overseas. In the case of the RMB, however, China assumes an active role in guiding the development of an offshore market with policies on, say, offshore RMB clearing banks, bilateral swap arrangement, and the QFI program. Does this state-driven approach affect the evolution of offshore RMB businesses?

Focusing on offshore currency trading, Table 2 gives the correlation estimates between an offshore center's share of total foreign exchange (FX) trading and its share of a specific SDR currency's offshore trading. Data derived from four recent BIS surveys (Bank for International Settlements, 2010, 2013, 2016, 2019)

---

[49] Hong Kong's role in promoting the international use of the RMB was noted as recently as in China's 14th Five Year plan for the period 2021–2025; the Chinese and English versions of the Five Year Plan are available from www.gov.cn/xinwen/2021-03/13/content_5592681.htm and https://cset.georgetown.edu/publication/china-14th-five-year-plan/, respectively.

Table 2 Correlation between trading shares of a specific SDR
currency and total FX

	2010	2013	2016	2019
USD	0.9997	0.9998	0.9996	0.9997
Euro	0.9897	0.9907	0.9810	0.9888
GBP	0.9796	0.9862	0.9862	0.9867
JPY	0.8911	0.9611	0.9188	0.9279
RMB	0.4719	0.4247	0.5257	0.4941

Note: For a given currency (column 1) and a given year (row 1), the table reports the correlation between a financial center's share of the currency's turnover and its share of total FX trading.

are used to generate these correlation estimates. Compared with the RMB, the other four SDR currencies – the US dollar, the euro, the British pound, and the Japanese yen – are established global currencies, albeit with different levels of prominence. They are also the top four most-traded currencies in the global foreign exchange market.

The correlation estimates of the RMB are different from those of the other four SDR currencies. Based on the BIS data, China's correlation estimates are noticeably below one, while the other four SDR currencies are quite close to one. That is, a financial center's share of global foreign exchange trading is quite closely associated with its trading shares of the US dollar, the euro, the British pound, and the Japanese yen. The geographic trading patterns of these four global currencies are similar around the world. However, the offshore RMB geographic trading pattern is different from the global foreign exchange trading pattern and those of the other SDR currencies.

While China grew both the scale and scope of offshore its RMB business worldwide in the 2010s, offshore RMB trading is quite highly concentrated. Table 3 shows the top four offshore RMB trading centers: Hong Kong, the United Kingdom, Singapore, and the United States. Hong Kong is the premier offshore RMB center and accounts for about 40% of offshore RMB trading in the four recent BIS surveys. The United Kingdom and Singapore alternate between the largest and the second-largest RMB trading center outside the Greater China region, while the United States follows closely behind. These four centers collectively account for more than 90% of the offshore RMB trading turnover. Considering the global importance of these four centers, Hong Kong and Singapore have a disproportionally high concentration of offshore RMB trading. The dispersion pattern is in accordance with China's strategy of leveraging the financial infrastructure of Hong Kong and prioritizing

Table 3 The top four offshore RMB FX trading centers (in percentages)

	Rank 1	Rank 2	Rank 3	Rank 4
2010	Hong Kong: 36.33	Singapore: 25.30	United Kingdom: 23.01	United States: 10.28
2013	Hong Kong: 43.38	United Kingdom: 21.29	Singapore: 20.92	United States: 7.56
2016	Hong Kong: 38.58	Singapore: 21.29	United Kingdom: 19.56	United States: 12.13
2019	Hong Kong: 41.41	United Kingdom: 21.80	Singapore: 16.38	United States: 11.49

Note: The first row lists the ranks of the top four offshore RMB FX trading centers reported in the BIS triennial surveys. The share of offshore RMB trading as a percentage is given next to the trading center's name.

regional use of the RMB over global use (Cheung 2015; Ehlers and Packer 2013; Ehlers, Packer and Zhu 2016). It also echoes the view that the RMB is still in the nascent stage of its internationalization process and in transit to be a fully globalized currency.

Cheung and Yiu (2017), Cheung, McCauley, and Shu (2019), and Cheung, Grimm, and Westermann (2021) investigate the factors affecting the geographic pattern of offshore RMB trading in the recent BIS surveys. Cheung and Yiu (2017) find that the swap line arrangement, the size of the financial markets, and the bilateral foreign direct investment flow affect the distribution of offshore RMB trading in the 2013 BIS survey.

Cheung, McCauley, and Shu (2019) show that China's RMB internationalization policy may have favored Asian financial centers such that in 2013 Asian financial centers including Hong Kong and Singapore had disproportionate shares in global RMB trading. But for the RMB to become a full-fledged global currency, its trading needs to gradually spread to other parts of the world according to market forces. Between 2013 and 2016, these authors found that offshore RMB trading seemed to converge to the spatial pattern of global foreign exchange trading; this transition was driven mainly by market forces and was not greatly affected by policies. Over the following three years – a period that witnessed an increase in geopolitical unrest – Cheung, Grimm, and Westermann (2021) find that, in addition to the reported convergence behavior, the evolution of offshore RMB trading was affected by (geopolitical) trade disputes and trade intensity. Further, the RQFII arrangement, equity market capitalization, and financial development played a role in shaping offshore RMB trading. These findings attest to the view that the forces that shape the geographical spread of RMB trading around the world can vary with the changing global economic and geopolitical environments.[50]

5 Current Status

Following the 2009 scheme of cross-border trade settlement in RMB, China has implemented various strategic reform measures to boost RMB usage in the global market. Anecdotal evidence indicates that China's concerted effort has made considerable headway in globalizing the RMB. The growing RMB business activities have gradually spread from the Asian region to other parts of the world. The emergence of the RMB as an upcoming global currency has raised a few eyebrows in the international community and triggered assessments and predictions about the prospects and consequences of internationalizing the RMB. The prognosis of RMB internationalization, mostly predicated on the basis of China's extraordinary growth and potential, abound.[51] In this subsection, we discuss a few quantitative measures of international RMB usage and its global status.

5.1 Share of Global Reserves

RMB's appointment as a member of the SDR basket is arguably the most recognizable achievement of China's efforts to internationalize its currency. The SDR is an international reserve asset created by the IMF. Being an SDR currency has positive implications for both passive and active demand for RMB as a global reserve currency.

Even before its SDR inclusion, there were a few predictions about RMB's role in global reserves. For instance, the Economist Intelligence Unit (2014) indicates that a majority of institutional investors – especially those within China – think that the RMB will overtake the US dollar as the main global reserve currency. Chen and Peng (2010), Hu (2008), and Lee (2014) suggest that, within 10 to 15 years, the RMB could account for 3–20% of global

---

50 Westermann (2021) shows that the geographic spread of offshore euro trading varies over time but exhibits patterns not identical to that of offshore RMB trading.
51 Chen and Peng (2010) offer an early assessment of a globalized RMB. Frankel (2012) assesses the RMB internationalization process in the context of other historical precedents. Eichengreen and Kawai (2015) collect articles discussing various issues related to RMB internationalization. Chen, Peng, and Shu (2009), Lee (2014), and Subramanian (2011a, b) suggest that the RMB was well prepared to be a main global currency, while Eichengreen (2013) and Yu and Gao (2011) express a more reserved view.

international reserves. Lu and Wang (2019) also find a wide range of predictions on the global reserve role of the RMB. This wide range reflects the sensitivity of the prediction to assumptions and methods used in these studies.

What is the RMB share of global reserves in the real world? Table 4 presents the global reserve holdings in the five SDR currencies. These data are extracted from the IMF Currency Composition of Official Foreign Exchange Reserves (COFER) database, which first identified the amount of global reserves held in the RMB in the last quarter of 2016.[52] The latest observation that is available at the time of writing is for the first quarter of 2021. The allocated data are compiled from those countries/jurisdictions that report the currency portfolios of their reserve holdings. The share of known currency allocation data gradually increased to about 94% in 2018 Q4 and has stabilized around that level since then. The US dollar and the euro are the two leading global reserve currencies; they account for 80–85% of allocated global reserves. The five SDR currencies collectively accounted for slightly less than 94% of allocated global reserves.

The RMB share of global reserves grew by 75% from 1.08% in 2016 to 1.89% in 2018, surpassed the Australian and Canadian dollars, and became the fifth largest reserve currency. The RMB share grew by 20% in the next two years to 2.27% by 2020 Q4, and a further 8% to 2.45% by 2021 Q1. More than 70 central banks and monetary authorities at the end of 2020 included the RMB in their reserve assets. (People's Bank of China 2021).

The growth of the RMB share of global reserves is quite impressive. Concurrently, the US dollar share of global reserves dropped from 65.36% in 2016 Q4 to slightly below 60% by 2021 Q1. It is not certain whether the RMB's inclusion in the SDR undercuts the primacy of the US dollar. Note that the euro, the Japanese yen, and the British pound also registered gains in their shares in global reserves during the same period.

Figure 9 plots the US dollar share of global reserves between 1965 and 2020. The US dollar share was above 80% in the 1970s and dropped below 50% in 1990 and 1991. Is the recent decline in the US dollar share part of its general cyclical movements or its secular downward trend? Arslanalp et al. (2022), for instance, show that the recent decline reflects active portfolio diversification by central bank reserve managers. It is worth noting that some countries have sought to diversify away from the US dollar. Russia, which has the fourth-largest holding of international reserves in the world, exemplifies this situation. It dramatically reduced the dollar share of its holding of international reserves from 45.8% to 22.7% between the beginning of 2018 and the beginning of 2021

---

[52] Since then, five SDR currencies and three non-SDR currencies have been "distinguished" in the COFER data. COFER compiles data reported from 149 countries and economies.

Table 4 Holdings of global FX reserves (billion US dollars); selected dates

	2016 Q4	2017 Q4	Q4 2018	Q4 2019	Q4 2020	Q1 2021
Total	10725.71	11457.43	11436.23	11827.04	12698.83	12570.60
Allocated	8418.16	10012.73	10727.09	11076.07	11871.00	11742.29
Unallocated	2307.54	1444.71	709.14	750.97	827.83	828.31
allocated/total (%)	78.49	87.39	93.80	93.65	93.48	93.41
USD	5502.07	6280.66	6623.43	6725.92	6996.36	6991.19
Euro	1611.03	2019.38	2217.58	2279.46	2526.78	2415.69
JPY	332.93	490.34	556.94	652.00	717.64	692.10
GBP	365.86	454.79	474.88	513.52	561.34	552.46
RMB	90.78	123.47	203.08	214.46	269.49	287.46
Allocated shares (%)						
USD	65.36	62.73	61.74	60.72	58.94	59.54
Euro	19.14	20.17	20.67	20.58	21.29	20.57
JPY	3.95	4.90	5.19	5.89	6.05	5.89
GBP	4.35	4.54	4.43	4.64	4.73	4.70
RMB	1.08	1.23	1.89	1.94	2.27	2.45
SDR-5	93.88	93.57	93.93	93.76	93.27	93.16
Other	2.33	2.43	2.47	2.53	2.66	2.74

Note: The breakdown of allocated global reserves in either billions of US dollars or percentages of total is listed. Data are from the COFER database.

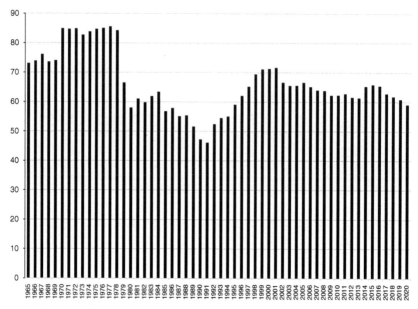

Figure 9 The US dollar share of allocated global official reserves (percentage)

Note: Data from COFER.

(Bank of Russia, 2019, 2020, 2021). By the beginning of 2021, Russia's international reserves held more gold (23.3%) than the US dollar. Russia's move away from the US dollar reduces the dollar share in global reserves.

Growth aside, the RMB share is small compared to the other four SDR currencies, especially the US dollar and the euro. Also, the amount of global reserves held in the RMB is comparatively minute. For instance, between 2016 Q1 and 2021 Q1, the global reserves held in dollars rose by US$1,489.12 billion, which is almost eight times more than the corresponding increase in the dollar value of global reserves held in the RMB and five times more than the total value of global reserves held in the RMB in 2021 Q1.

One caveat in reading these COFER data is the so-called valuation effect: the data are obtained from converting holdings of global reserves in different currencies into US dollars. Consequently, fluctuations of the US dollar exchange rate can affect the dollar share.

Further, China has incrementally disclosed the currency composition of its reserves holding to the COFER since 2015 Q2. The gradual disclosure can affect the currency composition of reported global reserves. The State Administration of Foreign Exchange of China (2019b, 2020, 2021) reports that China's holding of global reserves is more diversified than the world average; the US dollar accounted for 58% of China's global reserves in 2014 and 2015, and 59% in 2016, while the US dollar share of the world total was 65% in 2014 and 2016, and 66% in 2015. In these three years, China's holding of global reserves was between US$3.0 trillion in 2016 and US$3.8 trillion in 2014, while the total reported allocated global reserves were between US$6.8 trillion in 2014 and US$8.4 trillion in 2016. Given its relatively large holding, China's installment approach to reporting the currency composition of its international reserves holding can influence the reported US dollar share of global reserves.

5.2 FX Trading

International trade and finance transactions typically involve converting one national currency into another. Exchanges of national currencies are conducted in the global FX market, the world's largest decentralized financial market. Trading activity in the global FX market is a barometer for gauging a currency's prominence in the international monetary system. The BIS triennial central bank surveys present a detailed account of turnover in the global FX market. The surveys have documented the growing role of the RMB in the global FX market.

According to the surveys, the average RMB daily FX turnover volume in 2019 was US$285.0 billion, which is almost ten times its turnover volume of US$29.2 billion in 2010. The growth rate of the turnover was at a very high level of 300% between 2010 and 2013. It then slowed to 69% between 2013 and 2016 and 41% between 2016 and 2019. The RMB's global trading share has increased from 0.9% to 4.3% and improved from the 17th most traded currency to the 8th most traded one between the 2010 and 2019 BIS triennial surveys (Bank for International Settlements 2010, 2013, 2016, 2019).

Despite its rapid ascent in global FX trading, the RMB's turnover volume is still low compared with China's economic size and level of international trade. Table 5 lists the shares of global FX trading, ratios of average daily turnover to GDP, and ratios of average daily turnover to the international trade volume of the ten most traded currencies in the 2019 BIS survey.

There are a few observations. First, the RMB is the only developing economy currency on the top ten list. Second, the RMB ranks as the eighth most traded currency, while the other four SDR currencies are the top four. The US dollar, in particular, accounts for more than 80% of all transactions and has a turnover volume twenty times that of the RMB.[53] The RMB's turnover volume even lags

---

[53] Since two currencies are involved in each FX transaction, the sum of the percentage shares of individual currencies totals 200% instead of 100%.

Table 5 Average Daily FX Turnover, Economic Size, and Trade Volume.

	Turnover share (%)	Turnover/GDP (%)	Turnover/trade (%)
USD	88.3	28.0%	138.3%
EUR	32.3	15.8%	22.1%
JPY	16.8	22.4%	75.4%
GBP	12.8	29.7%	72.5%
AUD	6.8	31.3%	90.1%
CAD	5.0	19.5%	35.7%
CHF	5.0	46.7%	57.0%
CNY	4.3	2.1%	6.2%
HKD	3.5	63.7%	19.7%
NZD	2.1	66.8%	163.3%

Note: The table lists the shares of global FX average daily turnover, average daily turnover to GDP ratios, and average daily turnover to international trade ratios based on data from the Bank for International Settlements (2019), the IFS, and the IMF DOTS.

Australia, Canada, and Switzerland – countries that have a much smaller economy and trade sector.

Third, the turnover volume relative to GDP or relative to international trade shows a stark contrast between the RMB and the other top ten currencies. The columns for Turnover/GDP and Turnover/trade show that the RMB turnover is relatively low according to the GDP and trade volume economic measures. The RMB's ratios of average daily FX turnover to GDP and to international trade are noticeably smaller than the other ten most traded currencies. According to these two ratios, the New Zealand dollar is the most traded currency in the table, and the US dollar is arguably the most heavily traded currency among the SDR basket. The RMB has gained only a modest foothold in the global FX market by these counts.

China has promoted RMB trading in both the onshore and offshore markets. Onshore trading RMB is conducted on CFETS, the official onshore interbank platform established on April 18, 1994. In September 2015, China relaxed restrictions on foreign central banks, sovereign wealth funds, and international financial organizations to trade on CFETS. Since then, CFETS has steadily increased its trading members and opened the onshore interbank RMB market to authorized foreign participants. By the end of 2020, there were 735 authorized participants in the RMB spot trading market (People's Bank of China, 2021).

In addition, China has expanded direct trading of RMB against different individual currencies. Table 6 presents the currencies that are on the list of direct

Table 6 Currencies directly traded with the
RMB in CFETS

Starting date	Currency
August 2010	Malaysian ringgit
December 2010	Russian ruble
June 2012	Japanese yen
April 2013	Australian dollar
March 2014	New Zealand dollar
June 2014	British pound
September 2014	Euro
October 2014	Singapore dollar
November 2015	Swiss franc
June 2016	Korean won
June 2016	South African rand
September 2016	UAE dirham
September 2016	Saudi riyal
November 2016	Canadian dollar
December 2016	Hungarian forint
December 2016	Danish krone
December 2016	Polish zloty
December 2016	Swedish krona
December 2016	Norwegian krone
December 2016	Turkish lira
December 2016	Mexican peso
February 2018	Thai baht

Note: The table lists, besides the Hong Kong dollar
and the US dollar, the currencies that have official
direct bilateral currency trading arrangements with
the RMB in CFETS.

trading against the RMB.[54] In the second half of 2020, China waived interbank transaction fees between the RMB and twelve currencies – the Hungarian forint, Korean won, Malaysian ringgit, New Zealand dollar, Polish zloty, Russian ruble, Saudi riyal, Singapore dollar, South African rand, Thai baht, Turkish lira, and United Arab Emirates dirham – for three years to encourage direct trading with non-US currencies. With direct foreign exchange trading with non-US currencies, China can bypass the US dollar in settling cross-border transactions, lower currency conversion costs, and enhance international RMB use.

---

[54] Direct trading against the US and Hong Kong currencies was available before 2010. In addition to these currencies, the CFETS also supports regional trading of KZT, MNT, and KHR against the RMB.

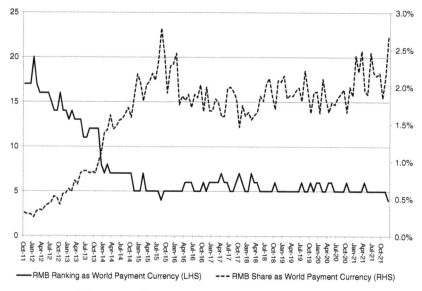

Figure 10 The RMB as a global payment currency
Note: Data from SWIFT RMB Tracker, various issues.

Note that the currencies that are directly tradable against the RMB under the CFETS platform match the component currencies of the CFETS RMB index.

Comparable to its offshore trading, the domestic RMB FX spot trading turnover increased from US$5.93 trillion in 2016 to US$7.9 trillion in 2019 and registered a 33% growth rate (People's Bank of China, 2017, 2020).[55] The RMB FX trading in both onshore and offshore markets is mainly against the US dollar – in both cases, trading against the US dollar in the past few years accounted for more than 90% of total turnover volume and is higher than the US dollar share (87.6% in 2016 and 88.3% in 2019) of global FX trading. While the RMB has established a foothold in the global FX market, its trading reflects the dominance of the US dollar.

5.3 Global Payment Currency

China is the second-largest economy and the largest trader in the world. In advocating the international use of the RMB, China emphasizes its role in facilitating trade and cross-border transactions. Figure 10 presents the data on the RMB usage for global payments by value from SWIFT (the Society for Worldwide Interbank Financial Telecommunication).

---

[55] The domestic RMB FX spot trading turnover was US$8.38 trillion in 2020 (People's Bank of China, 2021).

After touching a low rank of 20th and accounting for 0.25% of global payments in early 2012 (SWIFT, 2012), the RMB made strides to expand its role in cross-border payments. It became the 4th-ranked currency and accounted for 2.79% of global payments in August 2015 (SWIFT, 2015). Then, its ranking hovered between 5th and 7th until the second half of 2020, after which the share showed some upward momentum. In December 2021, the RMB scored the second highest share level of 2.70% and was ranked 4th. The performance of the RMB as a world payment currency reflects China's emphasis on trade facilitation and its substantial presence in international trade (SWIFT, 2022).

Undoubtedly, the RMB has secured a solid position in global payment usage. However, the RMB's share in world payments is still small compared with the US dollar and the euro. For instance, in December 2021, the US dollar and the euro accounted for, respectively, 40.51% and 36.65% of world payments. The RMB's 2.70% share of global payments is disproportionate to China's 17% share of the global GDP and 13% share of international trade.

5.4 Renminbi Globalization Index

Figure 11 presents the Renminbi Globalization Index (RGI) between December 2010 and October 2021. The Standard Chartered Bank launched the proprietary Index, which aggregates overseas RMB business activities, to obtain an operational measure of the level of RMB internationalization (Standard Chartered Bank, 2012). Starting with a base value of 100 in December 2010, RGI multiplied 25 times in slightly less than 5years to reach a height of 2,563 in September 2015. The increase in RGI reflects both the growth in the number of offshore financial centers included in the Index and the proliferation of RMB businesses in these centers.[56] The RGI movement attests the strong growth of international RMB usage between 2010 and 2015.

After September 2015, the RGI reversed its trend for about three years before resuming a steady upward trend in late 2018. The Index in March 2021 surpassed the September 2015 high and reached a new high of 2,698 in August 2021. It is perceived that the steady increase in the global use of the RMB is at least partially attributable to the resilience of the Chinese economy and the strength and stability of the RMB under the coronavirus pandemic (Standard Chartered Bank, 2021).

---

[56] The RGI initially covered only Hong Kong. It included Singapore and London in August 2011, Taiwan in July 2013, New York in January 2014, and Paris and Seoul in August 2014. The RMB activities covered by the Index include CNH deposits, cross-border payments, Dim Sum bonds and certificates of deposit issued, CNH turnover, and foreign holdings of onshore assets. See Standard Chartered Bank (2012, 2021) for additional information.

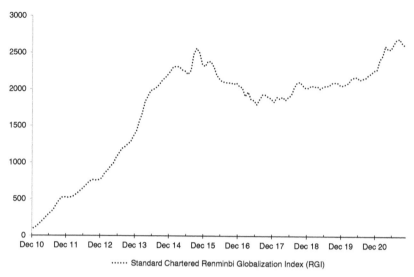

Figure 11 Renminbi Globalization Index, December 2010 to October 2021
Note: Data from Standard Chartered Bank.

5.5 Discussion

The preceding subsections show that China's state-led and assisted policies have propelled the RMB's penetration of the world economy. It has established positions in the areas of international reserves, global FX trading, and global transactions with an initially strong growth rate. The dynamics of the internationalization process have changed since late 2015. Specifically, around August 2015, data on both the SWIFT share of global payments and the Standard Chartered Bank RGI indicate that international RMB use dipped for a few years before regaining an upward – albeit weaker – momentum in 2019. At the same time, the RMB share of global reserves and global FX trading has also exhibited a weaker growth in the past few years. The expansion of the RMB into the global system is uneven over time and across areas.

The culprits behind the dip in international RMB use are the various unexpected foreign exchange and financial market management measures introduced after revamping the RMB central parity formation mechanism in August 2015. Without clear communications with the market, the authorities reined in capital outflows triggered by RMB depreciation expectations and financial deleveraging policy by fiat and hastily formulated policies. Among other things, these policies affected investment overseas and remittance of profits by foreign institutions. The abrupt implementation of these measures surprised foreign investors, who then had to reevaluate China's market reform policy and investment environment. To a certain extent, these administrative measures reinforce the perception of China's asymmetric policy framework of welcoming capital inflows while limiting outflows and highlight the risk of regulatory uncertainty.

The 2015 fiasco has created considerable uncertainty around China's financial liberalization policy and the RMB globalization process for foreign investors. It also has rekindled concerns about China's inextricable link of economic policy and political ideology. These unexpected policy measures highlight the deterring effects of nontransparent policies and capital controls on RMB use overseas and adversely affect the trust and confidence foreign investors have had in the global role of the RMB. After capital outflow stabilized, China relaxed restrictions on foreign investors participating in the bond, stock, and commodity futures markets to lure them back to these onshore markets. It also removed the quota limit of the RQFII program and introduced specific policies to promote onshore RMB trading.

The recent China–US trade dispute has further impeded the expansion of the RMB in the global market (Cheung, Grimm, and Westermann, 2021). The trade dispute not only affects China's trade and economic relationship with the United States, but also its relationships with US allies. And the effect has gone beyond the economic uncertainty associated with the resulting tariffs and restructuring of global supply chains: it has extended to conflicts in different areas, including technology and national security, that lead to strained geopolitical conditions – tensions which further hinder global usage of the RMB.

After a few years of sluggish development, the COVID-19 pandemic presented China with new opportunities to revive its RMB internationalization process. With its tenacious quarantine policy, China swiftly exited from pandemic lockdowns and asserted its resilience to the pandemic. Since the COVID-19 pandemic, China has increased its shares of world GDP and international trade. By successfully weathering the pandemic storm in late 2020 and 2021, China avoided quantitative easing policies and stabilized the RMB's value. China's resilient economy and stable currency form a formidable basis to advance the RMB internationalization process and attract foreign investors to RMB-denominated assets. Both the share of the RMB in global payments and the RGI registered gains in 2020 and 2021.

6 Geopolitics

Besides economic incentives, a globalized RMB offers China a financial apparatus for fortifying its global influence and the prestige of a globally significant country, and reduces its vulnerability to the US dollar. In addition to bolstering the RMB's role in international trade, global financial markets, and global reserves, China has pursued other strategies to strengthen its geopolitical weight and raise its status on the global stage. The improved geopolitical clout can, in turn, enhance the credibility and acceptability of the RMB and elevate its bargaining power with the United States.

Participation in international organizations provides a venue for a country to promulgate its views, influence others, and gain access to information about the latest economic and geopolitical developments. The role of a country in international organizations, especially those of global significance, reflects its global standing and prestige. After securing the status of the only legitimate representative to the United Nations in 1971,[57] China has actively and methodically joined international organizations, including those under supranational institutions such as the United Nations, the IMF, and the World Bank.[58] With its sizable shares of world GDP and global trade, China aspires to play a prominent role in international organizations. To that end, China has adopted a shrewd and schematic strategy of securing key positions in international organizations and showed how to use its growing economic clout to build a significant geopolitical force.

China has steadily increased its assertiveness and influence in international organizations, especially since showing its resilience to the 2007–8 GFC. For instance, in 2009 the then governor of the People's Bank of China, Zhou Xiaochuan, drew considerable global attention by implicitly challenging the US dollar hegemony. He suggested replacing a single super-sovereign reserve currency (the US dollar) with a supranational reserve currency (the SDR), in which the RMB should play a role (Zhou, 2009). His successor, Yi Gang, echoed the message and called for the allocation of the new SDR to cushion the adverse impact of the pandemic and support recovery (Yi, 2020).[59] The promotion of the SDR can be a disguised policy for undermining the primacy of the US dollar in the international monetary system and increasing the role of the RMB in global reserves.

In addition to pushing for a louder voice and a more significant role in existing international organizations, China is developing its own global economic and financial networks that mimic some existing organizations. Some

---

[57] On October 25, 1971, the United Nations General Assembly passed Albania's Resolution 2758 and replaced the Republic of China – the then representative of China – with the People's Republic of China.

[58] See *CIA World Factbook* at www.cia.gov/the-world-factbook/countries/china/#government and www.uscc.gov/prc-international-orgs.

[59] In August 2021, the IMF approved the allocation of about SDR 456 billion. Before 2021, there were four allocations: SDR 9.3 billion (1970–2), SDR 12.1 billion (1979–81), SDR 21.5 billion (August 10, 2009), and SDR 161.2 billion (August 28, 2009).

examples are the Asian Infrastructure Investment Bank, the Belt and Road Initiative, CIPS, the New Development Bank, and the Shanghai Cooperation Organisation. Apparently, China does not intend to replace the existing international organizations with these new establishments. However, these "sino-centric" organizations offer China alternative platforms to engage with the rest of the world and propagate its agenda without being constrained by the norms and restrictions of existing international organizations, which the US and its allies dominate.

China's admirable growth and resilience to both the 2007–8 GFC and the COVID-19 pandemic have steadily strengthened its geopolitical clout and bargaining power in the international community over time. It has gradually extended its political and economic influences and cultivated its credibility by participating in these existing and new international organizations. Besides advancing its influences and interests in the global arena, China's roles in these organizations help to enlist support for using RMB globally.

While China has actively advocated for international RMB use, some of its other policies are counterproductive. For instance, the revamp of the RMB daily fixing mechanism in 2015 and the subsequent measures on capital outflows illustrate the deterring effect of nontransparent policies on globalization of the RMB.

A recent example of China's counterproductive policies is its regulatory crackdowns on certain privately owned companies. Since the regulatory authorities abruptly suspended the mega IPO of Ant Financial in November 2020, the crackdown has subsequently affected corporations in the technology, education, and real estate sectors. These actions sparked volatile movements in Chinese equity prices in both onshore and offshore markets. The scale of this regulatory crackdown is unprecedented and caught most foreign investors off guard. While the objectives of these regulatory actions are understandable, investors are dismayed by the opaque policymaking process that led to these actions. The resulting market volatility does not bode well for foreign investors, worsens investment sentiment in Chinese equities,[60] and impedes international uses of the RMB (Standard Chartered 2021).

The RMB's global status depends on China's economic and political fundamentals, credibility, and global leadership, as perceived by foreign investors. Economic strength is an important factor but not the only concern determining the use of the RMB overseas. Despite China's growing economic prowess and rising geopolitical power, noneconomic factors not entirely controlled by China

---

[60] The investment sentiment is also impacted by the possible delisting of Chinese corporations by 2023 from the US exchanges if they do not provide US regulators with their audited accounts.

can dictate the evolution process of RMB internationalization. For instance, China's territorial disputes with neighboring countries, especially in the South China Sea, have revived antagonistic memories of historical territory disputes and ancient grudges.[61] The fatal confrontation at their disputed border in June 2020 escalated tensions between China and India – two established nuclear powers. These territorial disputes that mirror a legacy of previous conflicts undercut China's proclamation of a peaceful development strategy. The perceived military aggressiveness and image of regional hegemony do not help to persuade other countries to accept the global role of the RMB.

Does China's solid economic performance, especially during crisis periods, justify its major country status and new role in global affairs? In establishing its "major country diplomacy (*daguo waijiao* 大國外交 in Chinese)" or "great power diplomacy" with Chinese characteristics,[62] China displays implacable attempts to play down the Western economic and political values and develop a global and ideological environment favorable to its expansion. Its responses to perceived violations of its core interests by foreign governments and corporations can be assertive and confrontational. At times, the reaction to foreign critics and perceived slights is bellicose and aggressive. In addition to diplomatic protests and condemnation, there can also be trade sanctions, travel bans, and mass social media ridiculing the offending party. The combative approach is sometimes referred to as "Wolf Warrior" diplomacy.[63] Unsurprisingly, such belligerent and antagonistic behavior has provoked a backlash.

In recent years, China has engaged in diplomatic rows with some countries (including Australia, Japan, Korea, Singapore, and the United States) that have triggered economic and trade consequences. The Australia–China diplomatic row exemplifies the weaponization of trade policy for political disputes. Since Australia warned of China's growing influence on its politics in 2017, the diplomatic relationship between the two countries has become strained.[64] It reached a low point when Australia called for an investigation of the source of COVID-19 in 2020 (Trian, 2020). China has imposed sanctions and/or anti-dumping tariffs on beef, barley, coal, and wine and warned its citizens not to travel to Australia. China did not admit a connection between these sanctions and the diplomatic disputes. The sequence of events has dramatically altered Australia's view on China. For instance, Australia's trust in China fell to a new

---

[61] See, for example, Huang and Billo (2015). Stokes (2015) indicates that the territorial disputes undermined China's popularity in the region.

[62] Xi Jingping laid out the idea of major country diplomacy in his speech to the 2014 The Central Conference on Work Relating to Foreign Affairs.

[63] Some called it "coercive diplomacy" (Hanson, Currey, and Beattie 2020).

[64] Citing national security reasons, Australia banned the Chinese company Huawei from its 5G network project in 2018.

record low in a 2021 survey: only 16% of Australians say they trusted China "a great deal" or "somewhat" to act responsibly in the world, whereas 52% of Australians trusted China in the 2018 survey (Natasha Kassam, 2021),

The resentment at China's retribution against Lithuania illustrates a recent blowback from its policy of weaponizing trade. When Lithuania housed a Taiwanese Representative Office in 2021, China stoutly denounced the action and ferociously retaliated with economic coercion of unusual scope.[65] Both imports from and exports to Lithuania were literally halted. In addition, corporations, especially those in Europe, have been pressured to cut Lithuania from their supply chains. Similar to other political disputes, China did not formally declare any sanctions or punitive measures against Lithuania. In January 2022, the European Union lodged a complaint with the WTO over China's discriminatory trade practices against its member state Lithuania.

The assertive diplomacy with Chinese characteristics combined with weaponized trade policy can deliver a demonstration effect and direct other countries to respect China's core interest. On the other hand, the punishment diplomacy is likely to obliterate trust and credibility and forces countries to reassess the costs and benefits of close economic ties with China and the adoption of the RMB for cross-border business. Even though these diplomatic confrontations may be short lived, they can weaken commitments to adopting the RMB for international transactions.

Since Donald Trump entered the White House, the conflict between China and the United States has been the talk of the global community. The conflict reflects concerns about China's economic and political influences amid its assertiveness and global expansion. The China–US trade dispute is a case in point: the US has mounted pushback against China's (perceived) unfair trade expansion supported by state-led nonmarket practices (Mavroidis and Sapir, 2021). China's interactions with the rest of the world are affected by tariffs and global supply chain restructuring triggered by the trade dispute. The trade dispute is only one part of a larger China-US rivalry that encompasses multiple areas, including technology, finance, intelligence, influences in the Asia-Pacific region, and control of international organizations. The rivalry goes beyond disputes about economic issues in specific areas and has evolved into one between competing systems of values and ideologies: the United States seeks like-minded allies to contain China strategically, diplomatically, and economically.

---

[65] This harsh relationship is also founded on the Lithuanian parliament's decisions in May 2021 to label China's campaign against Uyghur Muslims as genocide and its call for China to rescind the national security law in Hong Kong.

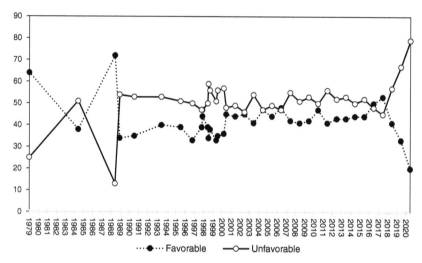

Figure 12 Views on China

Note: Data from Gallup poll surveys

The hostile rivalry with China and the unprecedented COVID-19 pandemic have negatively affected views on China in the United States. Gallup poll surveys demonstrate the evolution of the view of the US public on China. Figure 12 shows that the percentage of favorable views of China has declined from a recent high of 53% in 2018 to a historical low of 20% in 2021. At the same time, the level of unfavorable perception reached a historical high of 79%.[66]

This increasingly negative sentiment is also recorded by the 2021 PEW Research Center Survey that covers public opinion of China in seventeen advanced economies in North America, Europe, and the Asia-Pacific region (Silver, Devlin, and Huang, 2021). The percentage of respondents in the United States that have an unfavorable view of China steadily increased to 76% in 2021. Of the seventeen economies in the survey, Greece and Singapore are the only two with a percentage of unfavorable views below the 50% level. The economies that experienced various diplomatic and political disputes with China in the last few years, such as Australia, Japan, and South Korea, have a percentage of unfavorable views higher than that of the United States. The median percentage of unfavorable views across the seventeen economies is 69%.

---

[66] See https://news.gallup.com/poll/331082/china-russia-images-hit-historic-lows.aspx. The percentage of "favorable" views is the sum of those of the "very favorable" and "mostly favorable" views. The "unfavorable" views comprise "mostly unfavorable" and "very unfavorable" views. The choice of "no opinion" is available to respondents.

Such conflicts and the accompanying belligerent rhetoric give rise to geopolitical discord and volatile external market conditions for China. The pushback from the United States and other developed economies against China's economic practices and foreign policy further aggravated its external situations. The shift in geopolitical sentiment and attitudes toward China can, at least temporarily, adversely affect foreign investors' views on RMB-denominated assets and their commitment to support the internationalization of the RMB.

7 Concluding Remarks

China's remarkable and sustained economic growth bolsters its growing influence on the global stage. Its rise has fundamentally shifted the global balance of power between the East and the West, and has triggered the race for economic and geopolitical superiority. While economic clout constitutes a solid base buttressing China's geopolitical development and global reach, it is not the only factor. A case in point is the international use of the RMB.

When China kicked off its RMB internationalization program after the 2007–8 GFC, the world anxiously anticipated a global RMB that matches its economic might. In the early 2010s, the RMB appeared to be on its destined path to be a key global currency. However, the RMB internationalization process had stalled for a few years when it achieved a remarkable triumph and won SDR currency status in 2015. The process appears to have regained some advancement opportunities following China's resilience to the COVID-19 pandemic.[67]

Despite the rapid growth of the early 2010s and the steady improvement afterward, the role of the RMB in the global monetary system is relatively small and not commensurate with China's standing in the global economy. For instance, the RMB accounts for 4.3% of global FX trading (2019), 2.45% of global reserves (2021Q1), and 2.70% of world payments (2022M1). These shares are low compared with China's GDP and trade volume, which accounted for 17% and 13% of their respective world totals in 2020. These shares are also small compared with the other SDR currencies, especially the US dollar and the euro.

With its strong economic performance in recent decades, China is gaining confidence to act like a major country in the world. It has methodologically asserted its international role and global influences to match its economic and trade weights. Its remarkable economic prowess provides the potency of its RMB internationalization policy. Undoubtedly, the RMB is underrepresented in the global market and its global role does not match China's economic might. Why?

---

[67] The effectiveness and efficiency of China's resource-intensive zero-Covid policy were questioned in 2022, especially given the economic impact of mass testing and large-scale lockdowns in response to the contagious Omicron variant.

One observation is that, in the history of international finance, very few countries have been able to successfully make their currencies into a major global currency. Also, the process of replacing an incumbent global currency takes a long time and does not happen often. The last time it happened was when the US dollar replaced the British pound during the world wars of the twentieth century. Since then, there have been a few (unsuccessful) attempts – the Deutsche mark, the Japanese yen, and the euro – to challenge the US dollar's global dominance.[68] Even supported by China's global economic standing and tactical strategies, the RMB path to becoming a full-fledged global currency is a long process. Given China's track record of achieving trade dominance, there is reason to believe China contrived to internationalize the RMB with a similar gradualist approach that combines strategic market-oriented programs with state-led policies. Government controls and regulatory intervention are imposed when deemed necessary to maintain stability. However, the unexpected (though occasional) reversions to administrative foreign exchange and financial market controls have tended to erode the market's confidence and trust in the RMB's global role.

Another observation is that the US dollar has been the world's dominant global currency since the Second World War. The global primacy of the US dollar is not preordained. The United States has earned its primacy with its strong economic and political attributes, which include sophisticated financial markets, a transparent legal system, credible public institutions, and global economic and military leadership. The United States has maintained a flexible exchange rate with a convertible capital account, which enhances the acceptance of the US dollar overseas. Over time, the US dollar has earned substantial credibility and trust from the global community and has become a prominent international (reserve) currency. While some have noted that the Trump administration weakened the US global image and that US growth is now behind China's, it is uncertain whether these points grant the RMB a definite edge over the US dollar.

Some observers point out that China's capital controls and immature financial system limit international usage of the RMB. Outsourcing RMB businesses to offshore financial centers does not resolve all the issues associated with policy and domestic market constraints. There are concerns about the scope and the pace of China's reform programs. However, even without complete convertibility and exchange rate flexibility, foreign central banks have included RMB-denominated

---

[68] See Chinn and Frankel (2007), Eichengreen and Flandreau (2009), Franke (1999), Frankel (2012), Ministry of Finance of Japan (2003), and Takagi (2011). The euro attempt can be argued as an ongoing case (European Commission, 2018).

assets in their holdings of foreign reserves, and global investors have made RMB-denominated assets part of their portfolios. Anecdotal evidence suggests that, in addition to offshore RMB channels, China has continuously opened its domestic markets to foreign investors and financial institutions, albeit at its own pace.

Seemingly, capital controls and insufficient liberalization of the financial system alone are not entirely responsible for the slow progress of RMB internationalization. For instance, the historical capital control experiences of the pound sterling in the 1950s and the US dollar in the 1970s show that full convertibility is neither a necessary nor a sufficient precondition of a global currency. Of course, when most major currencies are largely convertible, the imposition of (unexpected) capital controls can erode a currency's global status.

Do the Chinese currency internationalization policies better the prospect of unfettered capital flows at market-driven exchange rates and convince the global community to generate sufficient demand for RMB-denominated assets? The RMB's global role has to be accepted by the world before it can become a major international currency. The global investor's acceptance of a globalized RMB depends on their confidence and trust in the currency. The confidence and trust the RMB earns in turn affect the rate at which it penetrates the international financial market and its prospect of becoming a key global currency. Confidence and trust are not derived only from economic strengths. They depend on, for example, policy transparency and predictability. Both the unexpected foreign exchange management measures following the 2015 exchange rate policy change and the 2020 regulatory crackdowns illustrate the effects of policy uncertainty on the confidence and trust of foreign investors.

While China's incredible economic progress has provided a solid base for globalizing the RMB, the internationalization process is hampered by the headwind from the deteriorating geopolitical environment. As discussed earlier, both China's actions and the policies of some developed countries contributed to the geopolitical tensions that have developed in the past few years. The China–US conflict manifests the differences in values underlying the Chinese economic and political model and the Western system. As China expands its influence globally, it is pushing for an environment that favors its continuous growth and challenges the existing global order. In recent years, the United States and its allies took different actions to rein in China's influence. In the world of realpolitik based on national interests and practical and material matters, the paths of mutual economic gain and national superiority can diverge. The China–US rivalry makes the global market less accommodating to China's state-led economic practices and subsequently weakens the international demand for RMB-denominated assets. Such geopolitical conflicts and anti-China rhetoric play a role in determining the path of the RMB internationalization process.

Moving forward, China's promising growth prospects and integration into the global economy can pull in global players to further the international use of the RMB, especially if it continues to liberalize its financial markets, enhance market liquidity, loosen its grip on the RMB, improve capital mobility, and enforce the rule of law. The presence of sophisticated financial markets, open public institutions, the rule of law, and trusted political systems are key factors underpinning a full-fledged global currency. The internationalization of the RMB is not an objective in itself but is the result of financial liberalization and global acceptance. To weaken or even reverse the dominant geopolitical headwinds, China has to be embraced by the global community, cooperate with the global system of values, and undertake international responsibilities in improving global security and governance.

The US dollar, which plays a prominent role in the global monetary system, definitely enjoys the so-called incumbency advantage. The prominence of the US dollar has reinforced the economic and political clout of the United States, and vice versa. China's gradualist approach, which takes the style of "subtlety, indirection, and the patient accumulation of relative advantage" that Henry Kissinger admired (Kissinger, 2011, p. 15), will likely deliver the tactically planned outcome and elevate the global stature of the RMB. The global role of the US dollar, on the other hand, is interwoven in the current global monetary system. The RMB, a relative new member of the global market, needs to gain the trust and the confidence of the international community to further its standing. The marketing of the RMB to the world must be met by international demand, which is limited though increasing. While the RMB is likely to surpass some SDR currencies in the near to medium future, the process of dethroning the US dollar may be a long one.

Appendix

Table A1 Offshore RMB clearing banks

Offshore Financial Center	Authorized Date	Authorized Bank
Hong Kong, China	December 2003	Bank of China, Hong Kong
Macau, China	September 2004	Bank of China
Taiwan	December 2012	Bank of China
Singapore	February 2013	Industrial and Commercial Bank of China
London, UK	June 2014	China Construction Bank
Frankfurt, Germany	June 2014	Bank of China
Seoul, South Korea	July 2014	Bank of Communications
Paris, France	September 2014	Bank of China
Luxembourg	September 2014	Industrial and Commercial Bank of China
Doha, Qatar	November 2014	Industrial and Commercial Bank of China
Toronto, Canada	November 2014	Industrial and Commercial Bank of China
Sydney, Australia	November 2014	Bank of China
Bangkok, Thailand	January 2015	Industrial and Commercial Bank of China
Kuala Lumpur, Malaysia	January 2015	Bank of China
Santiago, Chile	May 2015	China Construction Bank
Budapest, Hungary	June 2015	Bank of China
Johannesburg, South Africa	July 2015	Bank of China
Buenos Aires, Argentina	September 2015	Industrial and Commercial Bank of China
Zambia	September 2015	Bank of China
Zurich, Switzerland	November 2015	China Construction Bank
New York, US	September 2016	Bank of China
	February 2018	J. P. Morgan
Moscow, Russia	September 2016	Industrial and Commercial Bank of China

Appendix

Table A1 (cont.)

Offshore Financial Center	Authorized Date	Authorized Bank
Dubai, UAE	December 2016	Agricultural Bank of China
Karachi, Pakistan	May 2018	Bank of China
Tokyo, Japan	October 2018	Bank of China
	May 2019	MUFG Bank
Manila, Philippines	September 2019	Bank of China

Note: Information collected from Bloomberg, People's Bank of China, and the State Administration of Foreign Exchange of China.

Table A2 Bilateral RMB Currency Swap Agreements

Date	Counterparty	Amount
20-Jan-09	Hong Kong Monetary Authority	RMB200 billion and HK$227 billion
8-Feb-09	Bank Negara Malaysia	RMB80 billion and MYR40 billion
11-Mar-09	National Bank of the Republic of Belarus	RMB20 billion and BYR 8 trillion
23-Mar-09	Bank Indonesia	RMB100 billion and IDR175 trillion
2-Apr-09	Central Bank of Argentina	RMB70 billion and ARS38 billion
20-Apr-09	Bank of Korea	RMB180 billion and KRW38 trillion
9-Jun-10	The Central Bank of Iceland	RMB3.5 billion and ISK66 billion
23-Jul-10	Monetary Authority of Singapore	RMB150 billion and SG$30 billion
18-Apr-11	Reserve Bank of New Zealand	RMB25 billion and NZD5 billion
19-Apr-11	Central Bank of the Republic of Uzbekistan	RMB0.7 billion and UZS167 billion
6-May-11	Bank of Mongolia	RMB5 billion and MNT1 trillion
13-Jun-11	National Bank of Kazakhstan	RMB7 billion and KZT150 billion

Table A2 (cont.)

Date	Counterparty	Amount
26-Oct-11	Bank of Korea	RMB360 billion and KRW64 trillion
22-Nov-11	Hong Kong Monetary Authority	RMB400 billion and HK$490 billion
22-Dec-11	Bank of Thailand	RMB70 billion and THB320 billion
23-Dec-11	State Bank of Pakistan	RMB10 billion and PKR140 billion
17-Jan-12	Central Bank of the United Arab Emirates	RMB35 billion and AED20 billion
8-Feb-12	Bank Negara Malaysia	RMB180 billion and MYR90 billion
21-Feb-12	Central Bank of the Republic of Turkey	RMB10 billion and TRY3 billion
20-Mar-12	Bank of Mongolia	RMB10 billion and MNT2 trillion
22-Mar-12	Reserve Bank of Australia	RMB200 billion and AUD30 billion
26-Jun-12	National Bank of Ukraine	RMB15 billion and UAH19 billion
7-Mar-13	Monetary Authority of Singapore	RMB300 billion and SG$60 billion
26-Mar-13	Central Bank of Brazil	RMB190 billion and BRL60 billion
22-Jun-13	Bank of England	RMB200 billion and GBP20 billion
9-Sep-13	Hungarian National Bank	RMB10 billion and HUF375 billion
12-Sep-13	Bank of Albania	RMB2 billion and ALL35.8 billion
30-Sep-13	The Central Bank of Iceland	RMB3.5 billion and ISK66 billion
9-Oct-13	European Central Bank	RMB350 billion and EUR45 billion
25-Apr-14	Reserve Bank of New Zealand	RMB25 billion and NZD5 billion
18-Jul-14	Central Bank of Argentina	RMB70 billion and ARS90 billion

Table A2 (cont.)

Date	Counterparty	Amount
21-Jul-14	Swiss National Bank	RMB150 billion and CHF21 billion
21-Aug-14	Bank of Mongolia	RMB15 billion and MNT4.5 trillion
16-Sep-14	Central Bank of Sri Lanka	RMB10 billion and LKR225 billion
11-Oct-14	Bank of Korea	RMB360 billion and KRW64 trillion
13-Oct-14	Central Bank of the Russian Federation	RMB150 billion and RUB815 billion
3-Nov-14	Qatar Central Bank	RMB35 billion and QAR20.8 billion
8-Nov-14	Bank of Canada	RMB200 billion and CAD30 billion
22-Nov-14	Hong Kong Monetary Authority	RMB400 billion and HK$505 billion
14-Dec-14	National Bank of Kazakhstan	RMB7 billion and KZT200 billion
22-Dec-14	Bank of Thailand	RMB70 billion and THB370 billion
23-Dec-14	State Bank of Pakistan	RMB10 billion and PKR165 billion
18-Mar-15	Central Bank of Suriname	RMB 1 billion and SRD 520 million
25-Mar-15	Central Bank of Armenia	RMB 1 billion and AMD 77 billion
30-Mar-15	Reserve Bank of Australia	RMB200 billion and AUD40 billion
10-Apr-15	South African Reserve Bank	RMB 30 billion and ZAR 54 billion
17-Apr-15	Bank Negara Malaysia	RMB180 billion and MYR 90 billion
10-May-15	National Bank of the Republic of Belarus	RMB 7 billion and BYR 16 trillion
15-May-15	National Bank of Ukraine	RMB15 billion and UAH 54 billion
25-May-15	Central Bank of Chile	RMB 22 billion and CLP 2.2 trillion

Table A2 (cont.)

Date	Counterparty	Amount
3-Sep-15	National Bank of Tajikistan	RMB 3 billion and TJS 3 billion
26-Sep-15	Central Bank of the Republic of Turkey	RMB12 billion and TRY 5 billion
20-Oct-15	Bank of England	RMB 350 billion and GBP 35 billion
14-Dec-15	Central Bank of the United Arab Emirates	RMB35 billion and AED20 billion
7-Mar-16	Monetary Authority of Singapore	RMB300 billion and SG$64 billion
11-May-16	Bank Al-Maghrib, Morocco	RMB 10 billion and MAD 15 billion
17-Jun-16	National Bank of Serbia	RMB 1.5 billion and RSD 27 billion
12-Sep-16	Hungarian National Bank	RMB10 billion and HUF 416 billion
27-Sep-16	European Central Bank	RMB350 billion and EUR45 billion
6-Dec-16	Central Bank of Egypt	RMB 18 billion and EGP 47 billion
21-Dec-16	The Central Bank of Iceland	RMB3.5 billion and ISK66 billion
19-May-17	Reserve Bank of New Zealand	RMB25 billion and NZD5 billion
6-Jul-17	Bank of Mongolia	RMB15 billion and MNT5.4 trillion
18-Jul-17	Central Bank of Argentina	RMB70 billion and ARS175 billion
21-Jul-17	Swiss National Bank	RMB150 billion and CHF21 billion
27-Nov-17	Hong Kong Monetary Authority	RMB400 billion and HK$470 billion
8-Jan-18	Bank of Thailand	RMB70 billion and THB370 billion
30-Mar-18	Reserve Bank of Australia	RMB200 billion and AUD40 billion
3-Apr-18	Bank of Albania	RMB2 billion and ALL34.2 billion
11-Apr-18	South African Reserve Bank	RMB 30 billion and ZAR 54 billion

Table A2 (cont.)

Date	Counterparty	Amount
27-Apr-18	Central Bank of Nigeria	RMB15 billion and NGN720 billion
10-May-18	National Bank of the Republic of Belarus	RMB 7 billion and BYR 16 trillion
23-May-18	State Bank of Pakistan	RMB20 billion and PKR351 billion
25-May-18	Central Bank of Chile	RMB 22 billion and CLP 2.2 trillion
28-May-18	National Bank of Kazakhstan	RMB7 billion and KZT350 billion
20-Aug-18	Bank Negara Malaysia	RMB180 billion and MYR110 billion
13-Oct-18	Bank of England	RMB350 billion and GBP 40 billion
26-Oct-18	Bank of Japan	RMB200 billion and JPY3.4 trillion
19-Nov-18	Bank Indonesia	RMB200 billion and IDR440 trillion
10-Dec-18	National Bank of Ukraine	RMB15 billion and UAH 62 billion
11-Feb-19	Central Bank of Suriname	RMB 1 billion and SRD 1.1 billion
10-May-19	Monetary Authority of Singapore	RMB300 billion and SG$61 billion
30-May-19	Central Bank of the Republic of Turkey	RMB12 billion and TRY10.9 billion
8-Oct-19	European Central Bank	RMB350 billion and EUR45 billion
7-Dec-19	Macau Monetary Authority	RMB30 billion and MOP35 billion
10-Dec-19	Hungarian National Bank	RMB20 billion and HUF 864 billion
10-Feb-20	Central Bank of Egypt	RMB18 billion and EGP41 billion
20-May-20	Bank of Lao PDR	RMB6 billion and LAK7.6 trillion
31-Jul-20	State Bank of Pakistan	RMB30 billion and PKR720 billion

Table A2 (cont.)

Date	Counterparty	Amount
31-Jul-20	Central Bank of Chile	RMB50 billion and CLP5.6 trillion
31-Jul-20	Bank of Mongolia	RMB15 billion and MNT6 trillion
22-Aug-20	Reserve Bank of New Zealand	RMB25 billion
17-Sep-20	Hungarian National Bank	RMB40 billion
22-Oct-20	Bank of Korea	RMB400 billion and KRW70 trillion
25-Nov-20	Hong Kong Monetary Authority	RMB500 billion and HK$590 billion
8-Jan-21	Bank of Thailand	RMB70 billion and THB370 billion
13-Jan-21	Bank of Canada	RMB200 billion and CAD30 billion
22-Mar-21	Central Bank of Sri Lanka	RMB10 billion and LKR300 billion
15-Jun-21	Central Bank of the Republic of Turkey	RMB35 billion and TRY46 billion

Note: These agreements usually have a maturity of three years and are renewable. A few exceptions are the latest agreements with Korea, Hong Kong, Thailand and Canada, which have a five-year term. Information collected from Bloomberg, People's Bank of China, and the State Administration of Foreign Exchange of China.

References

Ahmed, S. (2009). Are Chinese Exports Sensitive to Changes in the Exchange Rate? *International Finance Discussion Papers No. 987.*

Aizenman, J. & Pasricha, G. K. (2010). Selective Swap Arrangements and the Global Financial Crisis: Analysis and Interpretation. *International Review of Economics & Finance,* **19**(3), 353–65.

Almas, I., Grewal, M., Hvide, M., & Ugurlu, S. (2017). The PPP Approach Revisited: A Study of RMB Valuation Against the USD. *Journal of International Money & Finance,* **77**(October), 18–38.

Arslanalp, S., Eichengreen, B., & Simpson-Bell, C. (2022). The Stealth Erosion of Dollar Dominance: Active Diversifiers and the Rise of Nontraditional Reserve Currencies. *IMF Working Paper WP/22/58.*

Assenmacher, K., Berentsen, A., Brand, C., & Lamersdorf, N. (2021). A Unified Framework for CBDC Design: Remuneration, Collateral Haircuts and Quantity Constraints. *ECBank Working Paper 2578.*

Bank for International Settlements. (2010). Triennial Central Bank Survey of Foreign Exchange and Derivatives Market Activity in 2010. Basel: Bank for International Settlements.

Bank for International Settlements. (2013). Triennial Central Bank Survey of Foreign Exchange and Derivatives Market Activity in 2013. Basel: Bank for International Settlements.

Bank for International Settlements. (2016). Triennial Central Bank Survey of Foreign Exchange and Derivatives Market Activity in 2016. Basel: Bank for International Settlements.

Bank for International Settlements. (2019). Triennial Central Bank Survey of Foreign Exchange and Derivatives Market Activity in 2019. Basel: Bank for International Settlements.

Bank of Russia. (2019). Bank of Russia Annual Report for 2018. Moscow: Bank of Russia.

Bank of Russia. (2020). Bank of Russia Annual Report for 2019. Moscow: Bank of Russia.

Bank of Russia. (2021). Bank of Russia Annual Report for 2020. Moscow: Bank of Russia.

Benassy-Quere, A., Lahreche-Revil, A., & Valerie, M. (2008). Is Asia Responsible for Exchange Rate Misalignments within the G20? *Pacific Economic Review,* **13**(1), 46–61.

Benkovskis, K. & Wörz, J. (2015). "Made in China" – How Does it Affect our Understanding of Global Market Shares? *ECB Working Paper 1787.*

Bergsten, C. F. (2007). The Chinese Exchange Rate and the US Economy. *Testimony before the Senate Committee on Banking, Housing & Urban Affairs,* January 31. www.piie.com/commentary/testimonies/chinese-exchange-rate-and-us-economy.

Bineau, Y. (2010). Renminbi's Misalignment: A Meta-Analysis. *Economic Systems,* **34**(3), 259–69.

Chen, H. & Peng, W. (2010). The Potential of the Renminbi as an International Currency. In W. Peng and C. Shu, eds., *Currency Internationalization: Global Experiences and Implications for the Renminbi.* London: Palgrave Macmillan, pp. 115–38.

Chen, H., Peng, W., & Shu C. (2009). Renminbi as an International Currency: Potential and Policy Considerations. *HKIMR Working Paper No.18/2009.*

Chen, J. (2013). Crisis, Capital Controls and Covered Interest Parity: Evidence from China in Transformation. In Y.-W. Cheung and J. De Haan, eds., *The Evolving Role of China in the Global Economy.* Cambridge, MA: MIT Press, pp. 339–71.

Chen, J. & Qian, X. (2016). Measuring On-Going Changes in China's Capital Controls: A De Jure and a Hybrid Index Data Set. *China Economic Review,* **38**, 167–82.

Chen, X. & Cheung, Y.-W. (2011). Renminbi Going Global. *China & World Economy,* **19**(2), 1–18.

Cheung, Y.-W. (2015). The Role of Offshore Financial Centers in the Process of Renminbi Internationalization. In B. Eichengreen and M. Kawai, eds., *Renminbi Internationalization: Achievements, Prospects, and Challenges.* Washington, DC: Brookings Institution Press, pp. 207–35.

Cheung, Y.-W., Chinn, M. D., & Fujii, E. (2007a). *The Economic Integration of Greater China: Real and Financial Linkages and the Prospects for Currency Union.* Hong Kong: Hong Kong University Press.

Cheung, Y.-W., Chinn, M. D., & Fujii, E. (2007b). The Overvaluation of Renminbi Undervaluation. *Journal of International Money & Finance,* **26**(5), 762–85.

Cheung, Y.-W., Chinn, M. D., & Nong, X. (2017). Estimating Currency Misalignment Using the Penn Effect: It is not as Simple as it Looks. *International Finance,* **20**(3), 222–42.

Cheung, Y.-W., Chinn, M. D., & Pascual, A. G. (2005). Empirical Exchange Rate Models of the Nineties: Are Any Fit to Survive? *Journal of International Money & Finance,* **24**(7), 1150–75.

Cheung, Y.-W., Chinn, M. D., Pascual, A. G., & Zhang, Y. (2019). Exchange Rate Prediction Redux: New Models, New Data, New Currencies. *Journal of International Money & Finance*, **95**(September), 332–62.

Cheung, Y.-W., Chow, K. K. & Qin, F. (2017). *The RMB Exchange Rate: Past, Current, and Future*; Singapore: World Scientific Publishing Co.

Cheung, Y.-W., Grimm, L., & Westermann, F. (2021). The Evolution of Offshore Renminbi Trading: 2016 to 2019. *Journal of International Money & Finance*, **113**(May), 102369.

Cheung, Y.-W. & He, S. (2022). RMB Misalignment: What Does a Meta-Analysis Tell Us? *Review of International Economics*, https://doi.org/10.1111/roie.12593.

Cheung, Y.-W. & Herrala, R. (2014). China's Capital Controls – Through the Prism of Covered Interest Differentials. *Pacific Economic Review*, **19**, 112–34.

Cheung, Y.-W., Hui, C.-H., & Tsang, A. (2018a). The Renminbi Central Parity: An Empirical Investigation. *Pacific Economic Review*, **23**(2), 164–83.

Cheung, Y.-W., Hui, C.-H., & Tsang, A. (2018b). The RMB Central Parity Formation Mechanism: August 2015 to December 2016. *Journal of International Money & Finance*, **86**(September), 223–43.

Cheung, Y.-W., Ma, G., & McCauley, R. N. (2011). Renminbising China's Foreign Assets. *Pacific Economic Review*, **16**(February), 1–17.

Cheung, Y.-W., Mccauley, R. N., & Shu, C. (2019). Geographic Spread of Currency Trading: The Renminbi and Other EM Currencies. *China & World Economy*, **27**(5): 25–36.

Cheung, Y.-W. & Qian, X. (2011). Deviations from covered interest parity: The case of China. In Y.-W. Cheung, V. Kakkar, & G. Ma, eds., *The Evolving Role of Asia in Global Finance*, Bingley: Emerald Group Publishing Limited, pp. 369–386.

Cheung, Y.-W. & Wang, W. (2020). A Jackknife Model Averaging Analysis of RMB Misalignment Estimates. *Journal of International Commerce, Economics & Policy*, **11**(2), 2050007.

Cheung, Y.-W. & Yiu, M. (2017). Offshore Renminbi Trading: Findings from the 2013 Triennial Central Bank Survey. *International Economics*, **152** (December), 9–20.

China Foreign Exchange Trade System. (2016). Public Announcement of China Foreign Exchange Trade System on Adjusting Rules for Currency Baskets of CFETS RMB Indices. www.chinamoney.com.cn/english/bmkidxrud/20161229/2050.html (updated November 2022).

Chinn, M. D. & Frankel, J. A. (2007). Will the Euro Eventually Surpass the Dollar as Leading International Reserve Currency? In R. H. Clarida, ed., *G7*

Current Account Imbalances: Sustainability and Adjustment, Chicago: University of Chicago Press, pp. 283–336.

Cline, W. R. (2015). Estimates of Fundamental Equilibrium Exchange Rates, May 2015. *Policy Brief 15-8*, Washington, DC: Peterson Institute for International Economics.

Cline, W. R. & Williamson, J. (2010). Estimates of fundamental equilibrium exchange rates. *Peterson Institute for International Economics Policy Brief No. 10–15*. Washington DC: Peterson Institute for International Economics.

Coudert, V. & Couharde, C. (2007). Real equilibrium exchange rate in China: Is the renminbi undervalued? *Journal of Asian Economics*, **18**(4), 568–594.

Cui, L., Shu, C., & Chang, J. (2009). Exchange rate pass-through and currency invoicing in China's exports. *HKMA China Economic Issues*, No. 2/09.

Ding, J. (1998). China's foreign exchange black market and exchange flight: Analysis of exchange rate policy. *The Developing Economies*, **36**(1), 24–44.

Dooley, M. P., Folkerts-Landau, D., & Garber, P. M. (2022). US Sanctions Reinforce the Dollar's Dominance. *NBER Working Paper No. 29943*.

Dornbusch, R. (1976). Expectations and exchange rate dynamics. *Journal of Political Economy*, **84**(6), 1161–1176.

Dunaway, S., Leigh, L., & Li, X. (2009). How robust are estimates of equilibrium real exchange rates: The case of China. *Pacific Economic Review*, **14**(3), 361–375.

Economist Intelligence Unit. (2014). Renminbi Rising: Onshore and Offshore Perspectives on Chinese Financial Liberalisation. An Economic Intelligence Unit report commissioned by State Street.

Ehlers, T. & Packer, F. (2013). FX and derivatives markets in emerging economies and the internationalization of their currencies. *BIS Quarterly Review*, December, 55–67.

Ehlers, T., Packer, F., & Zhu, F. (2016). The changing landscape of renminbi offshore and onshore markets. *BIS Quarterly Review*, December, 72–73.

Eichengreen, B. (2013). Renminbi internationalization: Tempest in a teapot? *Asian Development Review*, **30**(1), 148–164.

Eichengreen, B. & Flandreau, M. (2009). The rise and fall of the dollar (or when did the dollar replace sterling as the leading international currency?). *European Review of Economic History*, **13**(3), 377–411.

Eichengreen, B. & Kawai, M. (2015). *Renminbi Internationalization: Achievements, Prospects, and Challenges*. Washington, DC: Brookings Institution Press.

Engel, C., Lee, D., Liu, C., Liu, C., & Wu, S. P. Y. (2019). The uncovered interest parity puzzle, exchange rate forecasting, and Taylor rules. *Journal of International Money & Finance*, **95**(July), 317–331.

European Commission. (2018). Towards a stronger international role of the euro: Commission contribution to the European Council and the Euro Summit. https://ec.europa.eu/commission/publications/towards-stronger-international-role-euro-commission-contribution-european-council-13-14-december-2018_en.

Fernald, J., Hsu, E., & Spiegel, M. M. (2015). Is China Fudging its Figures? Evidence from Trading Partner Data. *Federal Reserve Bank of San Francisco Working Paper Series, Working Paper* 2015-12.

Fernández-Villaverde, J., Sanches, D., Schilling, L., & Uhlig, H. (2020). Central Bank Digital Currency: Central Banking for All? *NBER Working Paper No. 26753.*

Fischer, C. & Hossfeld, O. (2014). A consistent set of multilateral productivity approach-based indicators of price competitiveness: Results for Pacific Rim economies. *Journal of International Money & Finance,* **49**(December, Part A), 152–169.

Franke, G. (1999). The Bundesbank and the markets. In Deutsche Bundesbank, ed., *Fifty Years of the Deutsche Mark: Central Bank and the Currency in Germany since 1948.* Oxford: Oxford University Press, pp. 219–267.

Frankel, J. A. (2006). On the yuan: The choice between adjustment under a fixed exchange rate and adjustment under a flexible rate. *CESifo Economic Studies,* **52**(2), 246–275.

Frankel, J. A. (2009). New estimation of China's exchange rate regime. *Pacific Economic Review,* **14**(3), 346–360.

Frankel, J. A. (2012). Internationalization of the RMB and historical precedents. *Journal of Economic Integration,* **27**(3), 329–365.

Funke, M. & Gronwald, M. (2008). The undisclosed renminbi basket: Are the markets telling us something about where the renminbi–US dollar exchange rate is going? *The World Economy,* **31**(12), 1581–1598.

Funke, M. & Rahn, J. (2005). Just how undervalued is the Chinese renminbi? The *World Economy,* **28**(4), 465–489.

Garber, P. (2017). The geopolitics of ascending global currencies. In Y.-W. Cheung and F. Westermann, eds., *International Currency Exposure.* Cambridge, MA: MIT Press, pp. 289–296.

Garcia-Herrero, A. & Xia, L. (2015). RMB bilateral swap agreements: How China chooses its partners? *Asia-Pacific Journal of Accounting & Economics,* **22**(4), 368–383.

Goldberg, L. S. & Tille, C. (2008). Vehicle currency use in international trade. *Journal of International Economics,* **76**(2), 177–192.

Goldstein, M. & Lardy, N. (2009). *The Future of China's Exchange Rate Policy.* Washington, DC: Peterson Institute for International Economics.

Hanson, F., Currey, E. & Beattie, T. (2020). The Chinese Communist Party's Coercive Diplomacy. Policy Brief Report No. 36/2020. Australia: International Cyber Policy Centre at Australian Strategic Policy Institute.

Hinkle, L. E. & Monteil, P. J. (1999). *Exchange Rate Misalignment: Concepts and Measurement for Developing Countries*. New York: Oxford University Press.

Holz, C. A. (2004). China's statistical system in transition: Challenges, data problems, and institutional innovations. *Review of Income & Wealth*, **50**(3), 381–409.

Hu, F. (2008). The role of the RMB in the world economy. *Cato Journal*, **28**(2), 219–224.

Huang, H. & Wang, S. (2004). Exchange rate regimes: China's experience and choices. *China Economic Review*, **15**(3), 336–342.

Huang, J. & Billo, A. (2015). *Territorial Disputes in the South China Sea: Navigating Rough Waters*. London: Palgrave Macmillan.

International Monetary Fund Communications Department, (2015). IMF Staff Completes the 2015 Article IV Consultation Mission to China, *Press Release No. 15/237*, www.imf.org/external/np/sec/pr/2015/pr15237.htm.

Ito, T., Koibuchi, S., Sato, K., & Shimizu, J. (2010). Why has the yen failed to become a dominant invoicing currency in Asia? A firm-level analysis of Japanese Exporters' invoicing behavior. *NBER Working Paper* No. 16231.

Kassam, N. (2021). The 2021 Lowy Institute Poll, https://poll.lowyinstitute.org/report/2021.

Kawai, M. & Liu, L.-G. (2015). Trilemma challenges for the People's Republic of China. *Asian Development Review*, **32**(1), 49–89.

Kiff, J., Alwazir, J., Davidovic, S., et al. (2020). A Survey of Research on Retail Central Bank Digital Currency. *IMF Working Paper WP/20/104*.

Kissinger, H. (2011). *On China*. New York: Penguin Press.

Klein, L. & Ozmucur, S. (2003). The Estimation of China's Economic Growth Rate unpublished manuscript, University of Pennsylvania.

Koch-Weser, I. N. (2013). The Reliability of China's Economic Data: An Analysis of National Output, *US–China Economic & Security Review Commission Staff Research Project*.

Korhonen, I. & Ritola, M. (2011). Renminbi misaligned: Results from meta-regressions. In Y.-W. Cheung and G. Ma, eds., *Asia and China in the Global Economy*. Singapore: World Scientific Publishing Company, pp. 97–122.

Lai, E. (2021). *One Currency, Two Markets: China's Attempt to Internationalize the Renminbi*. Cambridge: Cambridge University Press.

Lee, J.-W. (2014). Will the Renminbi emerge as an international reserve currency? *The World Economy*, **37**(1), 42–62.

Liao, S. & McDowell, D. (2015). Redback rising: China's bilateral swap agreements and renminbi internationalization. *International Studies Quarterly*, **59**(3), 401–422.

Liew, L. H. & Wu, H. X. (2007). *The Making of China's Exchange Rate Policy*. Cheltenham: Edward Elgar.

Lin, G. & Schramm, R. M. (2003). China's foreign exchange policies since 1979: A review of developments and an assessment. *China Economic Review*, **14**(3), 246–280.

Lin, Z., Zhan, W., & Cheung, Y-W. (2016). China's bilateral currency swap lines. *China & World Economy*, **24**(6), 19–42.

Lu, Y. & Wang, Y. (2019). Determinants of Currency Composition of Reserves: A Portfolio Theory Approach with an Application to RMB. *IMF Working Paper WP*/19/52.

Ma, G. & McCauley, R. (2008). Efficacy of China's capital controls: Evidence from price and flow data. *Pacific Economic Review*, **13(1)**, 104–123.

Ma, G. & McCauley, R. (2011). The evolving renminbi regime and implications for Asian currency stability. *Journal of the Japanese and International Economies*, **25**(1), 23–38.

Mavroidis, P. C. & Sapir, A. (2021). *China and the WTO: Why Multilateralism Still Matters*. Princeton: Princeton University Press

Meese, R. A. & Rogoff, K. (1983). Empirical exchange rate models of the seventies: Do they fit out of sample? *Journal of International Economics*, **14** (1–2), 3–24.

Ministry of Finance of Japan. (2003). Promotion of the Internationalization of the Yen. Chairpersons' Report of Study Group on the Promotion of the Internationalisation of the Yen.

Miyashita, T. (1966). *The Currency and Financial System of Mainland China*. Seattle: University of Washington Press.

Morrison, W. M. & Labonte, M. (2013). China's currency policy: An analysis of the economic issues. Congressional Research Service.

Obstfeld, M. (2007). The Renminbi's dollar peg at the crossroads. *Monetary and Economic Studies*, **25**(S1), 29–55.

OECD. (2005). OECD Economic Surveys – China 2005. *Paris: Organization for Economic Cooperation and Development*.

People's Bank of China. (2005). Public Announcement of the People's Bank of China on Reforming the RMB Exchange Rate Regime, www.pbc.gov.cn/english/130721/2831438/index.html.

People's Bank of China. (2010). Further Reform the RMB Exchange Rate Regime and Enhance the RMB Exchange Rate Flexibility, www.pbc.gov.cn/english/130721/2845862/index.html.

People's Bank of China. (2015). The PBC Announcement on Improving Quotation of the Central Parity of RMB against US Dollar, www.pbc.gov.cn/english/130721/2941603/index.html.

People's Bank of China. (2017). 2017 RMB Internationalization Report, People's Bank of China.

People's Bank of China. (2020). 2020 RMB Internationalization Report, People's Bank of China.

People's Bank of China. (2021). 2021 RMB Internationalization Report, People's Bank of China.

Pethokoukis, J. (2014). Sorry, China, the US is still the world's leading economic power. *AEIdeas*, April 30, 2014. www.aei.org/publication/sorry-china-the-us-is-still-the-worlds-leading-economic-power/.

Prasad, E. S. (2016). The renminbi's ascendance in international finance. In R. Glick and M. M. Spiegel, eds., *Policy Challenges in a Diverging Global Economy*, San Francisco: Federal Reserve Bank of San Francisco, pp. 207–256.

Prasad, E. S. (2017). *Gaining Currency: The Rise of the Renminbi*. New York: Oxford University Press.

Prasad, E. S. & Wei, S.-J. (2007). China's approach to capital inflows: Patterns and possible explanations. In S. Edwards, ed., *Capital Controls and Capital Flows in Emerging Economies: Policies, Practices and Consequences*. Chicago, IL: University of Chicago Press, pp. 421–480.

Rawski, T. (2001). What is happening to China's GDP statistics? *China Economic Review*, **12**(4), 347–354.

Rawski, T. (2002). Measuring China's Recent GDP Growth: Where Do We Stand? *China Economic Quarterly*, **2(1)**, 53–62.

Rebucci, A. & Ma, M. (2019). Capital Controls: A Survey of the New Literature, *NBER Working Paper No. 26558*

Rosen, D. (1999). *Behind the Open Door: Foreign Enterprises in the Chinese Marketplace*, Washington, DC: Institute for International Economics.

Rossi, B. (2013). Exchange rate predictability. *Journal of Economic Literature*, **51**(4), 1063–1119.

Ruoen, R. & Kai, C. (1995). China's GDP in US Dollars Based on Purchasing Power Parity. *Policy Research working paper no. 1415*, Washington, DC: World Bank.

Schnabl, G. (2013). The role of the Chinese dollar peg for macroeconomic stability in China and the world economy. In Y.-W. Cheung and J. de Haan, eds., *The Evolving Role of China in the Global Economy*. Cambridge, MA: MIT Press, pp. 53–82.

Schnatz, B. (2011). Global imbalances and the pretence of knowing fundamental equilibrium exchange rates. *Pacific Economic Review*, **16**(5), 604–615.

Shi Lei 石雷. (1998). *Renminbi shi hua* (人民币史话). Beijing: Zhongguo Jinrong Chubanshe.

Silver, L., Devlin, K. & Huang, C. (2021). *Large Majorities Say China Does Not Respect the Personal Freedoms. of Its People*. Washington, DC: Pew Research Center.

Smith, R. C. (2016). Is China the next Japan? *The Independent Review*, **21**(2), 275–98.

Song, K. & Xia, L. (2020). Bilateral swap agreement and renminbi settlement in cross-border trade. *Economic and Political Studies*, **8**(3), 355–373.

Standard Chartered Bank. (2012). CNH – Introducing the Renminbi Globalization Index. Standard Chartered Bank: *Global Research*, November 14.

Standard Chartered Bank. (2021). Offshore Renbinbi – Subtle reassurance. Standard Chartered Bank: *Global Research*, November 16.

State Administration of Foreign Exchange of China. (2003a). Exchange Regulation for Border Trade (bianjing maoyi waihui guanli banfa) www.safe.gov.cn/model_safe/laws/law_detail.jsp?ID=80100000000000000,14&id=4.

State Administration of Foreign Exchange of China. (2003b). Notice for Issues relating to Domestic Institutions Using RMB as Denominated Currency in Foreign Trade (guanyu jingneijigou duiwaimaoyi zhong yi renminbi zuowei jijiahuobi youguanwenti de tongzhi) www.safe.gov.cn/model_safe/laws/law_detail.jsp?ID=80800000000000000,40&id=4.

State Administration of Foreign Exchange of China. (2019a). Abolish Restrictions on the Investment Quota of Qualified Foreign Investors (QFII/ RQFII) and Further Expand the Opening up of Financial Markets. www.safe.gov.cn/en/2019/0910/1552.html.

State Administration of Foreign Exchange of China. (2019b). State Administration of Foreign Exchange 2018 Annual Report. www.safe.gov.cn/en/2019/0905/1549.html.

State Administration of Foreign Exchange of China. (2020). State Administration of Foreign Exchange 2019 Annual Report. www.safe.gov.cn/en/2020/1221/1779.html.

State Administration of Foreign Exchange of China. (2021). State Administration of Foreign Exchange 2020 Annual Report. www.safe.gov.cn/en/2020/1221/1779.html.

Stokes, B. (2015). *How Asia-Pacific Publics See Each Other and Their National Leaders*. Washington, DC: Pew Research Centre.

Su, G. & Qian, J. (2021). Structural changes in the renminbi exchange rate mechanism. *China & World Economy*, **29**(2), 1–23.

Subacchi, P. (2016). *The People's Money: How China Is Building a Global Currency*. New York: Columbia University Press.

Subramanian, A. (2011a). Renminbi Rules: The Conditional Imminence of the Reserve Currency Transition. *Peterson Institute for International Economics Working Paper* No. 11–14.

Subramanian, A. (2011b). *Eclipse: Living in the Shadow of China's Economic Dominance*. Washington, DC: Institute of International Economics.

SWIFT. (2012). RMB Tracker – January 2012. SWIFT.

SWIFT, (2013). RMB Tracker – April 2013. SWIFT.

SWIFT. (2015). RMB Tracker – September 2015. SWIFT.

SWIFT. (2022). RMB Tracker – January 2022. SWIFT.

Sun, J. (2010). Retrospect of the Chinese exchange rate regime after reform: Stylized facts during the period from 2005 to 2010. *China & World Economy*, **18**(6), 19–35.

Takagi, S. (2011). Internationalizing the yen, 1984–2003: Unfinished agenda or mission impossible? In Y.-W. Cheung and G. Ma, eds., *Asia and China in the Global Economy*. Singapore: World Scientific Publishing Company, pp. 219–244.

The Economist (2014). Catching the eagle. The Economist, August 22, 2014. www.economist.com/blogs/graphicdetail/2014/08/chinese-and-american-gdp-forecasts.

Trian, N. (2020). Will souring China–Australia relations force a rethink on trade? *France24*, September 8, 2020. www.france24.com/en/20200908-could-souring-china-australia-relations-force-a-rethink-on-trade.

United States Department of the Treasury. (1992). Report to the Congress – Report to Congress on International Economic and Exchange Rate Policies, May 1992. *US Department of the Treasury, Office of International Affairs*.

United States Department of the Treasury. (1994). Interim Report to the Congress on International Economic and Exchange Rate Policies, July 1994. *US Department of the Treasury, Office of International Affairs*.

United States Department of the Treasury. (2006). Report to the Congress – Report to Congress on international economic and exchange rate policies, December 2006. *US Department of the Treasury, Office of International Affairs*.

United States Department of the Treasury. (2018). Report to the Congress – Macroeconomic and foreign exchange policies of major trading partners of the United States, October 2018. *US Department of the Treasury, Office of International Affairs*.

United States Department of the Treasury. (2019). Report to the Congress – Macroeconomic and foreign exchange policies of major trading partners of the United States, May 2019. *US Department of the Treasury, Office of International Affairs.*

Wang, Y., Hui, X., & Soofi, A. S. (2007). Estimating renminbi (RMB) equilibrium exchange rate. *Journal of Policy Modeling*, **29**(3), 417–429.

Westermann, F. (2021). On the Geographical Dispersion of Euro Currency Trading: An Analysis of the First 20 Years and a Comparison to the RMB. *HKIMR Working Paper* No. 25/2021

Working Group on E-CNY Research and Development of the People's Bank of China. (2021). Progress of Research & Development of E-CNY in China. www.pbc.gov.cn/en/3688110/3688172/4157443/4293696/2021071614584691871.pdf.

World Bank. (2013a). *China 2030*. Washington, DC: World Bank.

World Bank. (2013b). *Measuring the Real Size of the World Economy.* Washington, DC: World Bank.

World Bank. (2018). *Commodity Markets Outlook (October)*. Washington, DC: World Bank.

Wu, N. & Chen, Q. (2002). *Renminbi huilü yanjiu—xiudingben* (人民币汇率研究 – 修订本). Beijing: Zhongguo Jinrong Chubanshe.

Xu, Y. (2000). China's exchange rate policy. *China Economic Review*, **11**, 262–277.

Yi, G. (2020). The IMF should turn to special drawing rights in its Covid-19 response. *Financial Times – Opinion*, July 16. www.ft.com/content/e7efef20-3960-46e7-922b-112dba8f2def.

Yu, Y. & Gao, H. (2011). Internationalisation of the renminbi. In Y.-W. Cheung and G. Ma, eds., *Asia and China in the Global Economy*. Singapore: World Scientific Publishing Company, pp. 191–217.

Zhou, X. (2009). Reform the international monetary system. *BIS Review*, March 23. www.bis.org/review/r090402c.pdf.

Acknowledgement

I thank Paola Di Casola, Massimo Ferrari, Jorgo Georgiadis, Arnaud Mehl, Michele Ca' Zorzi, participants of the IPA economic meeting, ECB, Kenneth Reinert (Cambridge Elements in International Economics Series Editor), and two anonymous reviewers for their insightful and constructive comments, and David Wong and Yabin Wang for preparing the tables and figures. Also, I gratefully acknowledge the Hung Hing Ying and Leung Hau Ling Charitable Foundation for their continuing support.

Cambridge Elements ≡

International Economics

Kenneth A. Reinert

George Mason University

Kenneth A. Reinert is Professor of Public Policy in the Schar School of Policy and Government at George Mason University where he directs the Global Commerce and Policy master's degree program. He is author of *An Introduction to International Economics: New Perspectives on the World Economy* with Cambridge University Press and coauthor of *Globalization for Development: Meeting New Challenges* with Oxford University Press. He is also editor of *The Handbook of Globalisation and Development* with Edward Elgar and co-editor of the two-volume *Princeton Encyclopedia of the World Economy* with Princeton University Press.

About the Series

International economics is a distinct field with both fundamental theoretical insights and increasing empirical and policy relevance. The *Cambridge Elements in International Economics* showcases this field, covering the subfields of international trade, international money and finance, and international production, and featuring both established researchers and new contributors from all parts of the world. It aims for a level of theoretical discourse slightly above that of the *Journal of Economic Perspectives* to maintain accessibility. It extends Cambridge University Press' established reputation in international economics into the new, digital format of *Cambridge Elements*. It attempts to fill the niche once occupied by the *Princeton Essays in International Finance*, a series that no longer exists.

There is a great deal of important work that takes place in international economics that is set out in highly theoretical and mathematical terms. This new Elements does not eschew this work but seeks a broader audience that includes academic economists and researchers, including those working in international organizations, such as the World Bank, the International Monetary Fund, and the Organization for Economic Cooperation and Development.

Cambridge Elements $^{\equiv}$

International Economics

www.ingramcontent.com/pod-product-compliance
Ingram Content Group UK Ltd.
Pitfield, Milton Keynes, MK11 3LW, UK
UKHW020455010325
455719UK00016B/592